THE PRACTICE OF PRAYER

THE
PRACTICE OF PRAYER

BY

G. CAMPBELL MORGAN

BAKER BOOK HOUSE
Grand Rapids, Michigan

Reprinted 1971 by
Baker Book House Company
from the edition
published in 1960 by
Fleming H. Revell Company
in New York

Eleventh printing, July 1984

ISBN: 0-8010-5896-1

PHOTOLITHOPRINTED BY CUSHING - MALLOY, INC.
ANN ARBOR, MICHIGAN, UNITED STATES OF AMERICA

CONTENTS

CONTENTS

PRELIMINARY

"And it came to pass, as He was praying in a certain place, that when He ceased, one of His disciples said unto Him, Lord, teach us to pray, even as John also taught his disciples. And He said unto them, When ye pray, say, Father, Hallowed be Thy name. Thy kingdom come. Give us day by day our daily bread. And forgive us our sins; for we ourselves also forgive every one that is indebted to us, and bring us not into temptation.

"And He said unto them, Which of you shall have a friend, and shall go unto him at midnight, and say to him, Friend, lend me three loaves; for a friend of mine is come to me from a journey, and I have nothing to set before him; and he from within shall answer and say, Trouble me not; the door is now shut, and my children are with me in bed; I cannot rise and give thee? I say unto you, Though he will not rise and give him, because he is his friend, yet because of his importunity he will arise and give him as many as he needeth. And I say unto you, Ask, and it shall be given you: seek, and ye shall find: knock, and it shall be opened unto you. For every one that asketh receiveth; and he that seeketh findeth; and to him that knocketh it shall be opened. And of which of you that is a father shall his son ask a loaf, and he give him a stone? or a fish, and he for a fish give him a serpent? Or if he shall ask an egg, will he give him a scorpion? If ye then, being evil, know how to give good gifts unto your children, how much more shall your heavenly Father give the Holy Spirit to them that ask Him?"—
LUKE 11; 1-13.

I

PRELIMINARY

NEVER did the disciples prefer a more important request than when they said " Lord, teach us to pray " : and no petition was more graciously answered. The church to-day needs to bring that petition first of all, but she needs to do so remembering that she already has the answer in all spaciousness and clearness. Whatever may have been the case with the first disciples it is certainly true of us that before we " call " He " answers."

I have chosen as the general title of this book " The Practice of Prayer," because the purpose of its publication is preëminently practical. Any discussion of the doctrine of prayer which does not issue in the practice of prayer is not only not helpful, it is dangerous. At the same time that practice will be greatly helped by an apprehension of the relative Christian doctrine.

That there is need for its consideration is granted on every hand. Side by side with a great enrichment there is a wide-spread impoverishment in the Church of God. The consciousness of wealth creates the sense of poverty, and it is because we rejoice in our gain that we mourn over our lack.

As to enrichment, there can be no question that the church's appreciation of Jesus Christ is keener and more spacious to-day than it has ever been. There is to-day a wide-spread consciousness of the human Christ and this has brought assurance of His interest in all departments of human life. Coincidentally with this there has arisen a conviction of His universality, and while rejoicing as never in the warmth and nearness of the Flesh, we have come to a larger apprehension of the infinitude of the Word. In practical equipment for service too the Church in men, in money, and in methods, is far in advance of any preceding age.

Yet in all these things there is a sense of lack and of poverty. While the sense of the greatness of Christ is larger, the ability to bring men into loving, saving touch with Him sometimes seems less. The men at His disposal are many, but the Church lacks energy to send them forth. Money is more freely given than ever, and yet the greater part of the possessions of the saints is still retained for their own use. The methods are multiplied, and yet one cannot help the conviction that many of our organizations are fungus growths, sapping the Church's life and contributing nothing to her fruitfulness.

We are profoundly conscious of lack. Everywhere there is a double sense, that of power and of paralysis. We have heard the sound of the going in the top of the mulberry trees, but the wind of God seems to tarry. We saw the flaming of the bush among the Welsh mountains a little while ago, but we have not seen it in England. All about us are indifferent masses. We still mourn the dearth of conversions, and are painfully conscious of the languishing missionary spirit.

Where is the lack ? That is a larger question
than it is the purpose of this book to discuss.
Nevertheless, I think it may broadly be stated
that the supreme need of the Church is the realization experimentally of her relationship to God by
the Holy Spirit. In the interaction of life and
prayer will be found the secret of power, and the
realization of fellowship with God will never be
more than a theory save as prayer becomes a practice. I am particularly anxious to write nothing
censorious or that fails in recognition of all the best
things still to be found amongst us. I am profoundly conscious that there is a great deal of
prayer on the highest plane. God has His inter-
cessors everywhere. They are to be found often
in unexpected places, in men and women who
have learned the secret, and who by familiar intercourse with God are channels of blessing to
men; but the majority of us are not praying.
While I thank God for the prayers being offered
I feel that it is of the utmost importance that the
whole Church should know the secret of prevailing prayer, not only as a theory, but in practice.

In the presence of this need the importance of
our presenting the same petition as the early disciples is apparent. That petition must be carefully
understood. It was a much larger one than we too
often make it. We minimize its meaning by adding to its words. They did not say, Lord, teach us
how to pray, but, " Lord, teach us to pray." A
great many people know how to pray, but they do
not pray. The request, Teach us how to pray,

would refer simply to the theory. The petition "teach us to pray," is of much fuller import and includes theory and practice.

It is interesting to notice the circumstances in which the disciples preferred this request. "And it came to pass, as He was praying in a certain place, that when He ceased, one of His disciples said unto Him, Lord, teach us to pray." It is hardly possible to read these words without seeing the connection between their request and their observation of the Lord. Jesus Himself was preëminently a Man of prayer, and there is no doubt that they had often seen Him at prayer, in all probability had heard Him. Although He never prayed with them or used of His own prayers the same words He used of theirs, yet it was clearly manifest to them how much prayer meant to Him, and it is as though they had said, "We would come into this secret of Thine." It was a request arising from their conviction of the value of prayer in His life.

The answer of Jesus was far more comprehensive than at first sight may appear. Immediately He gave them a pattern and a parable. The pattern itself was not exhaustive, for it consisted of the recitation of certain sentences from the form of prayer included in His Manifesto. He then gave them a parable which taught by contrast the readiness of God to hear and answer. If through importunity, is the argument they could be persuaded to give, how much more would God give out of the love of His heart.

This pattern and parable, however, constitute nothing more than the local, immediate and partial answer of Jesus to their request. Later He gave them much detailed teaching in His paschal discourses, and yet not even this final teaching exhausted His great and gracious answer. He is Himself, in His revelation of the place and power of prayer in human life, the supreme answer to their request. By the whole fact of incarnation and perfect life, of atonement, resurrection and perpetual priesthood does Christ answer this preliminary prayer.

It is well for us to remember that we are in direct succession to these disciples, that their requests are our requests, and His answers to them are His answers to us. Making all allowance for a distinguishing between things which differ, between matters which pertain to the specific message of the early days of Jesus and matters connected with the commission under which we serve; it still remains true that His essential teaching was intended for us as well as for those who first heard it. When He stood surrounded by that first group of disciples He prayed, and in the course of His prayer He said, "Neither for these only do I pray, but for them also that believe on Me through their word." I always feel warmly near to the heart of Christ when I read these words, for I know that He saw me also, and included me in His priestly intercession. As there He prayed for us with them, so also in all His teaching He spoke to us as to them.

THE POSSIBILITY OF PRAYER

" He that cometh to God must believe that He is, and that He is a rewarder of them that seek after Him." —HEBREWS 11 : 7.

" If ye abide in Me, and My words abide in you, ask whatsoever ye will, and it shall be done unto you."—JOHN 15 : 7.

" And they continued stedfastly in the Apostles' teaching and fellowship, in the breaking of bread and the prayers."—ACTS 2 : 42.

II

THE POSSIBILITY OF PRAYER

WHILE the purpose of the present series of studies is that of stating the positive truth of the Christian faith concerning prayer, it is necessary at least to recognize the fact that among the things of weakness characterizing our age is a far spread doubt of the possibility of prayer. It is affirmed that the advance of scientific knowledge has made it impossible to believe that the desires and petitions of individual souls or of companies in agreement can have any effect upon the affairs of a universe conditioned absolutely within law. Some there are, therefore, and those the more consistent, who bandon prayer in every form, while others urge the maintenance of the habit of prayer because of the effect it produces upon those who pray. These claim that prayer, while devoid of objective value, has yet a subjective value. It is not my purpose to attempt any philosophical discussion on this question. I believe that the majority of persons who read will concede at once the objective value of prayer, and I do not think anything said in defense of the theory will bring conviction to those in doubt. It is only by praying that the possibility is proven. He has proved the objective value of prayer who has asked and received, who has sought and found, who has knocked and known the door opened in answer. Yet there are certain of the simplest things which may be said in this connection.

Let it once be granted that prayer has a subjective value and it will be difficult to escape conviction of its objective value. If it be true that petition has produced an effect upon character which is uplifting and ennobling, then that effect is due to belief in the existence of One who hears and is able to grant requests. If there be no such possibility, then belief in that which is untrue issues in character which is true and beautiful. This is unthinkable. All the subjective value of prayer has grown out of conviction of an objective value. If a man asks for something, it is because he believes he can obtain it by asking. Once persuade a man that it is impossible for him to receive an answer to his petition and he will not persist in asking. Thus will the subjective value of prayer be inevitably destroyed when the objective value is denied. No man will continue to ask if he be once convinced that his asking has no greater value than that it produces an effect upon himself. Everything which man has observed of the subjective value of prayer, of the influence it has produced upon character and tone, has been due to profound conviction of its objective value. Sincere and honest men who once deny the objective value cease praying, witness such men as Darwin, Tyndal, Spencer and Huxley. Their philosophy led them to the conclusion that prayer was never answered and therefore they properly and honestly—though as we think—mistakenly and disastrously ceased to pray.

I am not for a single moment denying the subjective value of prayer. No human being has ever lived the life of familiarity with the secret place without bearing the light and glory of it on the face. Those who know what it is to talk often with God gain a tone in their talking with men which cannot be mistaken. Herein the subjective value of prayer, but it came out of profound conviction that when they spoke they were heard, when they asked they were answered. I believe therefore that the demonstration of the subjective value of prayer is presumptive evidence of its objective value.

Our belief, however, in the prevailing power of prayer has firmer foundations. It is based first of all upon our doctrine of God. We do not believe that He is the slave of His own laws. At the same time we do not believe in a God who is lawless, but law-abiding. His knowledge of all law is, however, such as to enable Him in the overruling of one law by another so to perform what to our limited vision appears to be miraculous. Our doctrine of God makes us believe that it is possible for Him to do in answer to prayer that which appears to be contrary to law, but which is in reality wrought by the operation of a law of which we know nothing in relation to another law of which we know something. It is

reasonable that those who deny the possibility of
prayer always deny the existence of the miraculous. What is a miracle? The word simply
means something which surprises, something for
which we cannot account. Now, the only reason
why men deny the possibility of prayer is that
they deny the possibility of things which they
cannot understand. That is the meaning of the
denial of everything which we call supernatural.
Our doctrine of God affirms that from the standpoint of His existence, of His government, of
His love, there is nothing supernatural. The
things which appear to be supernatural to me,
are natural to Him. Every miracle of the New
Testament and of the Old Testament was a simple happening which surprised men who did not
know all the facts and forces of the universe.
Those things surprising to finite men were actions
perfectly natural to God. It is surely time that
we recognize this. A great many things of which
our fathers would have spoken as being quite as
miraculous as anything recorded in the Bible, are
commonplaces of every-day life to us. We are
not surprised at the wonders wrought by elec-
tricity because we have discovered laws of which
our fathers knew nothing. Yet the increase of
our knowledge makes us the more ready to declare that even to-day we are but children of the
dawn. The Christian affirmation is that God
dwells in the light and there is no darkness with
Him. That which appears to contradict nature
is in harmony with the whole economy of God,

and the work of God within the realm of laws
higher than those which man has yet discovered.
It may be objected that law cannot overrule law;
but experience proves the contrary. I hold a
book in my hand. The law of gravitation demands its fall but it remains in my hand because
of the operation of an overruling law. In all the
simplest things of life this inter-action of law is
at work. Now, the Christian doctrine of God
declares that He sitteth at the centre of the universe. He rules eternity with His presence. All
laws are but His thoughts, and He is able to call
into operation force against force, law against
law. We therefore believe it is possible for His
children to go to Him and ask of Him and receive
from Him things they cannot obtain in any other
way. Things absolutely impossible to men within
the realm of the laws they know may become
possible to them, if they can gain His ear and
touch His Heart and find the answer of His overruling power. Once deny that God can answer
prayer, and He is degraded into a being less than
His universe, a prisoner in the heart of His own
creation.

Again, our belief in the possibility of prayer is
based upon the declarations of Jesus, and behind
His declarations there is Himself. If when I ask
I never have ; when I seek I cannot find ; when
I knock no door is opened to me, then either
Christ was deceived or a deceiver. His teaching
was most explicit. In this connection one quota-
tion, perhaps the most remarkable of all, will

suffice. "If ye abide in Me, and My words abide
in you, ask whatsoever ye will, and it shall be
done unto you." A careful examination of that
passage makes it even more wonderful than appears at first sight. The word "ask" may with
perfect accuracy be rendered "demand as your
due." No violence will be done to the Lord's
words if instead of "whatsoever ye will" we read
"whatsoever ye are inclined to." Yet again, the
word translated "done," may be changed into
"generated," and we have here as it seems to me,
the most stupendous statement regarding prayer
ever uttered. It makes prayer limitless within
limits. "If ye abide in Me, and My words abide
in you," are the limits. Let these be observed,
then prayer becomes the method of coöperation
with Deity. The life of true relation to Himself is
one in which desire harmonizes with the purposes
of God, and which therefore demands an answer
which is provided even though the creative force
of Deity should be employed. If there is no
answer to prayer, then these are the words of
One who was deceived, or was a deceiver—impossible alternatives despite a thousand new-born
philosophies. Neither was He deceived, nor a
deceiver. What He said is true though the
heavens fall. Heaven and earth may pass away,
but His word cannot. To deny the possibility of
prayer is to deny the teaching of Jesus. To deny
that teaching is to destroy Him.

Yet once again, we base our belief in the possibility of prayer upon the history and experi-

ence of men. When science makes experience the universal test of reality how can men rationally exclude the experience of the saints of all ages in this matter? They tell us they have asked and had; sought and found; knocked and the door has been opened. In answer to this it is affirmed that they were all perfectly sincere in believing so, but they were mistaken. Such a statement is a test of patience to which I am not equal. To be told that not one or two; but hundreds, thousands, tens of thousands of human beings, not of one age or temperament or geographical position; but in every age, of all temperaments and from every clime, though weeks and months and years and decades and centuries and millenniums, have all been deceived, is to be asked to believe something far more incredible than anything which Christianity affirms as true. If the testimony of seers, prophets, psalmists, saints, confessors and martyrs is all to go for nothing; yet may God help me to share their delusion, for it has been a glorious delusion and the dynamic by which all the best work of the centuries has been done. We affirm therefore, our belief in the objective value of prayer, first because of our doctrine of God; secondly because of the declarations of Jesus Christ, and finally because of the history and the experience of the saints.

Yet, let me go one step further. God has been reached always through His Son, Jesus Christ. Not that men have always understood this, not that we perfectly understand it to-day, but the fact remains that fallen man has always found his way to God in prayer through the mystery of the mediation of Christ.   Now, that is the theme we are proposing to follow.   The Christian revelation is that of the constant method by which man has been able to pray ; by which man has asked and received, has sought and found ; has knocked and found the door opened.   So that the final proof of the objective value of prayer lies in all that Christian economy which we claim creates its possibility, and which is to be considered.

THE PLATFORM OF PRAYER

"*No man hath seen God at any time; but the only begotten Son, which is in the bosom of the Father, He hath declared Him.*"—JOHN 1: 18.

"*He that cometh from above is above all; he that is of the earth is of the earth, and of the earth he speaketh: He that cometh from heaven is above all. What He hath seen and heard, of that He beareth witness; and no man receiveth His witness. He that hath received His witness hath set His seal to this, that God is true.*"—JOHN 3: 31-33.

"*I am the good Shepherd: the good Shepherd layeth down His life for the sheep. . . . Therefore doth the Father love Me, because I lay down My life, that I may take it again. No one taketh it away from Me, but I lay it down of Myself. I have power to lay it down, and I have power to take it again. This commandment received I from My Father.*"—JOHN 10: 11, 17, 18.

"*Verily, verily, I say unto you, He that believeth on Me, the works that I do shall he do also; and greater works than these shall he do: because I go unto the Father. And whatsoever ye shall ask in My name, that will I do, that the Father may be glorified in the Son. If ye shall ask Me anything in My name, that will I do.*"—JOHN 14: 12-14.

"*And I will pray the Father, and He shall give you another Comforter, that He may be with you forever, even the Spirit of truth: whom the world cannot receive; for it beholdeth Him not, neither knoweth Him: ye know Him; for He abideth with you, and shall be in you. . . . But the Comforter, even the Holy Spirit, whom the Father will send in My name, He shall teach you all things, and bring to your remembrance all that I said unto you.*"—JOHN 14: 16, 17, 26.

"*But when the Comforter is come, whom I will send unto you from the Father, even the Spirit of truth, which proceedeth from the Father, He shall bear witness of Me.*"—JOHN 15: 26.

III

THE PLATFORM OF PRAYER

HAVING considered the subject of the possibility of prayer generally, we now proceed to think of it particularly, and as within the Christian fact. In the three groups of Scriptures with which this study is prefaced we have indicated the threefold fact which creates the possibility of prayer according to Christian teaching and experience. The selection of verses is not intended to be exhaustive. It would be quite possible to take other single verses containing the same truth in some other setting. It is also self-evident that in this study there is no intention of dealing exhaustively with the verses selected. I propose only to deduce from them their suggestiveness on this particular subject of prayer.

In the first place let me state the general value of each group. In the first our Lord is presented to us as the One who has revealed the Father. In the second He is presented as the One who brings us, through His mediatorial work, into the presence of the Father that there we may appear complete in the Son, and therefore unafraid. In the third He is presented to us as the One through whose perfect and accomplished work the Spirit is given to us to abide with us, to be in us.

This threefold fact creates the Christian platform of prayer. Its first phase is that Christ has made such a revelation of the Father as creates in our hearts a desire for prayer. The second is that He has done such work for us as admits us to the presence of God in order that we may have the right to pray. While the third is that upon the accomplishment of His work and as its crowning glory He poured forth His Spirit who by indwelling is the inspiration of our prayer as we stand in Christ in the presence of that God whom Jesus has perfectly revealed.

The relation of this threefold fact to our previous study should be noted. Therein we declared that we believe prayer to be possible because of our doctrine of God. From whence did we obtain this doctrine? From Christ's revelation of the Father. We declared in the second place, that we believe prayer to be possible because of the teaching of Christ. What was the final teaching of Christ in answer to that request of His disciples? It was not the teaching of His words, but that of His work. The meditation of Jesus is His ultimate teaching which brings conviction to our hearts of the possibility of prayer. Finally, we declared that we believe in the possibility of prayer because of the experience of the saints. How has that experience been created? It has ever been the result of the indwelling and inspiration of the Holy Spirit.

Let us now approach the subject from another standpoint, by asking whether prayer is possible

apart from these truths. I unhesitatingly reply
that it is not. If they are denied prayer will
cease sooner or later. There may be prayer in
some senses apart from a consciousness of these
things. There is an instinct for prayer in human
nature which expresses itself among all peoples ;
but prayer, as we understand it, as our fathers
have experienced it, and as the New Testament
teaches, is absolutely impossible save on that
platform. Let us begin with the first fact. Suppose it were possible to blot out the revelation
of God which the word has received through
Jesus Christ. The supposition is of course an
absurdity. The revelation can never be entirely
lost. It has become ingrained in the common
consciousness of the age. Those who deny the
deity of Jesus and tell us they believe in the
Fatherhood of God speaking with exquisite
beauty of that fatherhood, are speaking of that
which Christ revealed. For the sake of argument,
however, let us suppose it possible that the world
should lose that consciousness of God which
Christ has created, what then would be the result ?
The measure of intellectual progress apart from
revelation would be the measure in which men
would cease to pray. It may be objected that
this is to declare that prayer is not an intellectual
exercise, but that is not so. When I refer to the
measure of man's intellectual progress apart from
revelation I am proposing to omit the quantity
without which the intellect is at once darkened
and imprisoned. No man is a full grown intel-

lectual who is not ready to receive revelation. To turn the back upon revelation is necessarily to cease to pray. Why did Huxley, Tyndal, Darwin and Spencer cease to pray? The answer inevitably is, because they ceased to believe in revealed religion; they denied that God had revealed Himself to men directly and specifically. Some declared that He was unknowable, that it was not possible for Him to reveal Himself to men or for men to receive any revelation from Him. Denying revealed religion, they turned to nature and prosecuted their inquiry with absolute honesty and splendid devotion. Some of their number, as we well know, who in their early days possessed a love of poetry and music, lost it entirely in their devotion to cold scientific investigation. What was their ultimate position? They could not pray. And this, because nature never reveals that fact concerning God which creates desire for prayer. Nature does reveal God, but not in all the facts of His Being. What can a man find in nature if he shuts the book of revelation, and declines to believe that God has spoken in His Word or through His Son? The Apostle, writing to the Romans, declared that God had evidently revealed Himself in nature in two particulars, namely in His power and divinity. The men to whom reference has been made declared that they found at the back of all natural phenomena an eternal energy. One of them spoke of this as "a double-faced somewhat, a combination of intelligence and force." I accept the testimony of the Apostle and of the modern scientist, that you find God in nature as force and as intelligence, but to neither of these, nor to the two in cooperation, is it possible to pray. I cannot pray to force. All I can do in its presence is to discover its law and obey it in order that I may constrain it to serve me rather than to blast me. It is a perpetual law of force that it will do the one or the other according to the relation which we bear to it. Take dynamite as expressive of force. To disobey its law is to be scattered by it into fragments. By obedience to its law is the rock blasted and the highway created. When men would use dynamite they do not pray to it. They discover its law. If God be only an eternal energy, then I cannot pray, but even then I will attempt to discover the law of His operation and obey it. During the last fifty years man's conception of the divine intelligence has been greatly enlarged. As man has prosecuted his inquiry and come to understand more perfectly the marvel of the universe in the midst of which he lives, he has come to a larger comprehension of the marvel of the all-governing intelligence. For instance, there was a time when man turned his telescope to the heavens and counted the stars. A little later on with a more powerful instrument he declared that the number was far in excess of that first affirmed; until at last Rosse turned his great refractor to the heavens and declared that the stars cannot be counted. That is the scientific posi-

c

tion to-day. The Bible affirmed it long ago.
Jeremiah sang that the stars were without number, but men declared it was the license of poetry.
As a matter of fact it was cold, hard, scientific
fact. To return, however, this scientific investigation has enlarged man's conception of the intelligence behind nature, and in that proportion
it has been less easy for man to pray. That may
sound a strange thing to say, and yet I think it
must be conceded as true. When I find illimit-
able intelligence ordering seasons and mar-
shalling stars I cannot believe that by any asking
of mine I can hope to affect or persuade such a
mind. I cannot pray to intelligence.

But now I read " No man hath seen God at
any time; the only begotten Son, which is in the
bosom of the Father, He hath declared Him."
Here is a new quantity, a new fact, "the bosom
of the Father." Put this into other words and
read, "the heart of God." Jesus has revealed
the fact that God is more than force and intelli
gence working in coöperation. He is a persona.
Being, and at the back of the force presiding
over it, behind the intelligence inspiring it, is
love. If that be true there is at once born
within me a desire to pray. If it be true that
behind all the rest there is a heart, then I will
pray in spite of force, and notwithstanding intelligence. If God is but another name for intelligence, that intelligence is demonstrated to be so
stupendous that it is unthinkable and foolish for
me to attempt to pray to such a mind as that.

Prayer is impossible. I am bruised and broken upon life's highway but there is no help for me in the inscrutable might and mind of which I am conscious. But out of the infinite spaces there comes to me a great love song. Out of the bosom of the Father comes a message of tenderness and compassion. Immediately, bruised and broken as I am, I want to pray. I desire to speak out of my sense of sin and sorrow to the heart behind force and intelligence concerning my need. Agony can sob itself out upon a heart. Impotence can trust love. A sinner can turn his face back towards a Father. Neither force nor intelligence, nor both working in coöperation constitute God. If that is all a man knows of God he will cease to speak of it as God, and presently will write the word with a small g, or he will simply use the word in accommodation to the age in which he lives, not because of its personal significance. Christ has revealed to men the fact that the personality behind the universe is force, intelligence and heart, a complete personality, not only volitional and intellectual but emotional withal. While I cannot comprehend Him nor encompass Him within my finite thinking, I still know that I have found in that infinite conception something which perfectly corresponds to my finite life. There is something in me of force and intelligence, but the greatest of me is my heart. When my finite heart finds the infinite heart of God I am able to trust my finite strength to His infinite strength, and my finite mind to His infinite intelligence. This then is the first fact in the platform of prayer, that the God of the universe has a bosom, a heart, and that the Son has spoken to men out of it. By the way of Jesus Christ there has come to man this new revelation concerning God, the revelation of His heart, of His essential essence, of His love. Out of that revelation is born the passion for prayer in the soul of man.

Yet that fact alone does not make prayer possible, neither does it reveal to us the platform upon which we stand to pray. Though I appear to contradict what I have already said it must be affirmed that in the moment when I stand face to face with God as the God of love, even though the desire to pray is born within me I am conscious that I dare not pray. When Jesus Christ brings me into His presence and I find His love, there is immediately in my nature a going out after Him; but simultaneously with the birth of desire comes a new consciousness which seals my lips. It is when I stand in the presence of God as love that I realize for the first time the real meaning of sin, and I am silent. This assertion may not carry conviction at first, yet think of it! The men who have missed the vision of God's love have invariably lost their sense of their own sin. Those who have lost the God of revelation never speak of sin as do those who live in the light of revelation. Sin to the former is an infirmity, a weakness, a process of development. It has recently been affirmed that this is an age

in which men of highly developed intelligence
do not care to think of or speak of sin, but it is
surely no proof of high development that men
desire to close their eyes to facts. I repeat, that
to lose the vision of God is to lose the sense of
sin. If I simply think of an eternal energy
working in response to supreme intelligence, I
become conscious of my own weakness and my
own foolishness, but never of my sin. It is when
I stand in the presence of the heart of God that
I really begin to know what sin is. To illustrate
briefly from personal experience. I was born in
a Christian home, nurtured by Christian parents,
and by that fact graciously and tenderly spared
from many of the vulgarities of godlessness.
Consequently Mount Sinai with its thunder
never made me tremble, never brought deep conviction of sin to my heart. I have always sym-
pathized with the young ruler who confronted
by the six final words of the decalogue, could
yet look into the face of incarnate purity and
say, " All these things have I observed from my
youth." But when I came to stand consciously,
not at the foot of the mount which might not
be touched, but on the green hill outside the city
wall, and saw in the mystery of that passion and
pain the revelation of the heart of God, the self-
sacrificing, self-denying heart of God, I knew
what a sinner I was. When I came into the
presence of God as love I found in love a light
which bowed me to the dust in shame, and
though my sad heart yearned to pray, I dared

not take His name upon my lips, for He is **love** ineffable who has—let me say it reverently—denied Himself in order to help men. In the light of that love I discovered that sin does not consist in incidental acts of passing days, but in the essential attitude of selfishness. It is when Jesus brings me into the presence of the heart of God that I put my hand upon my lips and cry, Unclean, unclean. I want to pray. I dare not pray. I have forfeited all right to ask for anything from such love. I need yet more than the revelation of the Father before I can pray. Thank God there is more.

I pass to the second group of Scriptures and in them I find the provision I seek. "I am the good Shepherd: the good Shepherd layeth down His life for the sheep." Death and resurrection are in that sentence. He layeth down His life, that is the mystery of His dying. He layeth down His life for the sheep, that is, in such a way that it becomes communicate to them. "No one taketh it away from Me, but I lay it down of Myself. I have power to lay it down, and I have power to take it again. This commandment received I from My Father." Thus in the radiant splendour of these words of Jesus I see One who comes out from God, lays down His life, and in the mystery of that act clears me from sin, who takes His life again in resurrection and in the might of that act places at my disposal a new life which makes it possible for me to stand unafraid in the presence of God. All this is exactly what I need. I cannot pray unless my sin is forgiven and my dead

spiritual nature is brought to life. Hear me in
solemn reverence as I speak out of my heart's
deepest consciousness. I need something done
for me whereby the pollution of sin can be blotted
out, if not for God's sake for my own. If you
could persuade me that God could forgive me
without all that the Cross means, you could not
persuade me that I could forgive myself. I must
have something that cleanses from the pollution
which spoils and harms and clings to my life.
Sentimental passion and pity cannot purge the
stain from my own conscience. In the very deepest of me there is a cry which answers the very
word of revelation, " Without the shedding of
blood there is no remission." Ere I can enter the
presence chamber of the revealed Father and
pray, I need some mystery of cleansing and healing, some new dynamic which should touch and
quicken into life the withered powers within me.
I am amazed at the love of God, but I dare not
pray until the revealing Son stands before me as
Mediator also. "Who is this that cometh from
Edom, with dyed garments from Bozrah? this
that is glorious in His apparel, marching in the
greatness of His strength?" It is One with
wounded hands, the mystery of pain written upon
His face, with all the evidences of the passion of
sacrificial dying enwrapping Him as with a pur-
ple robe. Who is He? He is the Son, the good
Shepherd. The One who came after lost ones.
The One who found them bruised and broken;
mangled and torn by wolves. The One who laid
down His life to rescue them, and yet in such

power as to be able to take it again and communicate it to them so that it became their life. The One who by such dying and living has given to men of His life the vision, the virtue, the victory. It is God Himself acting out in the limitation of time and sense and flesh that infinite mystery of love saving through sacrifice. Thus it is through the rent veil of His flesh that I enter the place of prayer. It is through the mystery of His accomplished work that I dare to draw near. I who had felt the moving of God's heart as Jesus spake and taught and yet was made afraid thereby because of sin, am now brought near by the mystery of mediation and in the presence of God I dare to pray, standing unafraid in the light of God's love in the merit and might of the death and resurrection of His Son.

And yet once again, I cannot pray. The love of God revealed has made me desire to pray. The work of Jesus as Mediator has brought me into the place of prayer, but I was never more afraid to pray than now. That is the meaning of the Apostolic declaration, " We know not how to pray as we ought." For who are these of whom he thus speaks ? They are the people whose experience is described in the chapter which commences with "no condemnation," and ends with " no separation." There is surely no time in which a man feels less able to pray than when having seen the vision of God through Jesus, and having been made nigh by Jesus to God, he stands in the place where he is free to pray. The nearer we live to the heart of Jesus, and the closer we

abide in the consciousness of God's love the less
shall we feel able to pray.   We sometimes sing

> The weakest, feeblest need the most
> The praying in the Holy Ghost.

That is a great truth, and yet I think it may be
written in another way,

> The strongest, mightiest need the most
> The praying in the Holy Ghost.

That is to say those who have answered the revelation of love by absolute abandonment to the
mediating Son; those who have entered most
perfectly into the experience of the Divine provision, need most sorely a true inspiration, and
are the most acutely conscious of their need.   To
stand in the presence of such love by such grace
is to shrink back lest by some impurity of motive
or faultiness of desire prayer should become un-
worthy.

Thus we are brought to the third fact in the
provision for prayer, that was dealt with in the
final discourses of Jesus when He promised the
Comforter.   The indwelling Spirit interprets to
us the meaning of the life we live and gives us to
see the will of God in Jesus, and the way in
which we must act in order to realize that will.
The indwelling Spirit who knows the will of God
creates our new aspirations and desires, and out
of these comes our prayer.   Thus standing in the
light of the revealed Father through the mediation of His Son and answering the inspiration of
the indwelling Spirit we pray.

In conclusion let these thoughts be summarized.

By the coming of Jesus God has been so revealed
as to create the desire for prayer. By the work
of Jesus mediation has been made which brings
man into the place of prayer. By the indwelling
of Jesus by the Spirit desires are created and
choices are made which express themselves in
prayer. Thus through the mercy of the Father,
the merit of the mediating Son, and the might of
the inspiring Spirit, prayer is possible. That conception of the platform of prayer must have an
effect upon our praying. If we lack that vision we
shall pray ignorantly and foolishly. We shall
ask and have not because we ask amiss. If once
that platform of prayer be recognized and we un
derstand to whom, and through whom and by
whom we pray, our praying will become prevailing. The whole truth may be constantly remembered by the Apostolic benediction, "The grace
of the Lord Jesus Christ, and the love of God,
and the communion of the Holy Spirit." The
only difference is that in this benediction we commence with the grace of the Lord Jesus Christ
and then pass to that infinite fountain, the love
of God, and finally refer to that abiding fellowship, the communion of the Holy Spirit. "The
grace of the Lord Jesus Christ," "though He was
rich, yet for your sakes He became poor, that ye
through His poverty might become rich." That
is the story of mediation. "The love of God,"
that is the whole word of Christ's revelation.
"The communion of the Holy Spirit," that is the
fact of the Spirit's indwelling and inspiration.

THE PREPARATION FOR PRAYER

" Fear not, little flock ; for it is your Father's good pleasure to give you the Kingdom."—LUKE 12 : 32.

" But of Him are ye in Christ Jesus, who was made unto us wisdom from God, and righteousness and sanctification, and redemption."—1 CORINTHIANS 1 : 30.

" For we know that the whole creation groaneth and travaileth in pain together until now. And not only so, but ourselves also, which have the first-fruits of the Spirit, even we ourselves groan within ourselves, waiting for our adoption, to wit, the redemption of our body. For by hope we were saved ; but hope that is seen is not hope : for who hopeth for that which he seeth ? But if we hope for that which we see not, then do we with patience wait for it. And in like manner the Spirit also helpeth our infirmity : for we know not how to pray as we ought ; but the Spirit Himself maketh intercession for us with groanings which cannot be uttered ; and He that searcheth the hearts knoweth what is in the mind of the Spirit, because He maketh intercession for the saints according to the will of God. And we know that to them that love God all things work together for good, even to them that are called according to His purpose."—ROMANS 8 : 22-28.

IV

THE PREPARATION FOR PRAYER

LET me at once clear the ground by making plain what I do not mean by preparation for prayer. In this title there is no reference to any preparation which is occasional and special. For such preparation there will be no necessity in proportion as the larger preparation of the life is assured. It is a great question whether the attitude of mind which demands some recall and readjustment in order to public or private prayer is at any time one which is honouring to our Lord and Master. I am perfectly well aware that this is a somewhat startling statement, and I appeal for a careful consideration of the subject now to be dealt with that the truth concerned, may be ascertained. In the meantime I do most confidently affirm that it ought to be a perfectly natural and easy thing to turn from work or play to prayer at any time or in any place, and moreover, it seems to me increasingly, as days pass on that any work or play which makes that spontaneous prayer impossible should be abandoned at all costs and once for all. As to private prayer, believing as I do in its required constancy I cannot also believe in the necessity for any process of preparation. As to public prayer, an illustration will express in the simplest way my entire feeling on the subject. Some few years ago in a certain city in England, which shall be nameless, in preparation for special services I met the ministers and workers in conference. In the course of an address to them I said that I should be very glad if my brethren in the ministry would be on the platform with me and be ready to lead in prayer as they were asked. At the close of the meeting one minister came to me and said, "I should be so glad if you think of asking me to pray if you will let me know the day before so that I may be prepared." I replied, "If I want you to pray I will let you know the day before." I never asked him to pray. Some may object to this, believing that a man ought to have time to prepare to pray on such an occasion. I can only say for myself that the kind of preparation which has been very largely followed in any such case has in my judgment wrought wide-spread harm. At many of our great ecclesiastical gatherings, prayers are heard which are perfect literary productions, but which lack the passion and power which prevail. Consequently I am not dealing with the subject of how to prepare for prayer upon some special occasion. If we learn the deep secrets of prayer we shall be able to pray anywhen and anywhere. We shall fulfill the injunctions of the New Testament which startle us—Christ's injunction, "Men ought always to pray," and the Apostolic injunction, "Pray without ceasing." Too often our method of dealing with such texts is a revelation of our unprepared-

ness for prayer. We say Christ did not really
mean that men ought always to pray. He meant
that they ought to pray as often as they can. He
meant nothing of the kind. When He said,
"Men ought always to pray," He meant it.
When the Holy Spirit speaking through the
Apostle said "Pray without ceasing," He meant
it. If we can but learn the true secret of preparation we shall find that our whole life becomes
prayer, that it will be impossible for us to write
a letter without a lifting of the heart to God for
guidance. I am inclined to think that the more
we know of real prayer the less time we may
spend in the external and apparent exercise
thereof.

I am speaking then of the preparation which
touches life, and so makes us ready for prayer at
all times. Having thus attempted to clear the
ground let me proceed. I propose first to put
the whole statement into one brief sentence, and
then examine that sentence in detail. The whole
case then may thus be stated.

Preparation for prayer is secured by response
in the life to the great facts which make prayer
possible.

That I maintain is the inclusive philosophy of
preparation for prayer. Now let us examine that
statement. First of all it must be remembered
that all truth is a light which reveals a pathway
in which man must walk. Truth always sets up
a claim, makes a demand. It is never merely a
commodity which can be stored and labelled and

shelved. A man cannot hold truth. Truth must hold the man. Immediately truth presents itself to a life it makes a demand upon that life. While that is so in regard to all truth it is preeminently the case in regard to spiritual truth. Every truth of the Christian faith taken hold of by the mind makes a call upon the will. In proportion as that claim is answered the life is sanctified. I hold the truth which holds me. Take that principle and apply it to this subject of prayer. We have seen that the platform of prayer consists of the threefold fact of the revelation of the Father, the mediation of the Son, the inspiration of the Spirit. I am prepared for prayer in proportion as I obey the claims set up upon my life by the revelation of the Father; in proportion as I yield myself to the claims made upon my life by the mediation of the Son; in proportion as my life answers the claims set up within me by the Spirit's indwelling and inspiration. I see the truth about God revealed in Jesus and that truth makes claims upon me. If I answer them I am by such answer prepared for prayer. I am brought into the place where I see the truth concerning Christ's great mediatorial work. If I answer the claim that truth makes upon me I am prepared for prayer. I see the truth concerning the Spirit's method of making intercession. If I answer that indwelling illumination, yield myself to it, refuse to quench, or resist or grieve the Spirit, and allow my life to be borne along by the great currents of the river of God, I shall be prepared to pray, bound to pray, and shall always pray. In other words, preparation for prayer is the life lived in harmony with the truth we profess to believe. It is not spasmodic, occasional; but lies rather in the preparation of the life itself and in proportion as we are living as we ought to live, we not only want to pray, we are able to pray : we not only want to pray and are able to pray, but we do pray, and that so as to prevail.

Let us consider this more particularly by application of the principle in the case of the previous study, our platform of prayer. We saw it to be of threefold significance, including the revelation of the Father, the mediation of the Son, the inspiration of the Spirit. If it be true that we are prepared for prayer as we respond to the great truths suggested by those words, we now have to ask ourselves, " What is the revelation of the Father ; what the mediation of the Son ; what the inspiration of the Spirit ? " We need to examine these things in order to find out how far we are responsive to them, how far we are obedient, so that thus we may find out how far we are really prepared for prayer. Such questions, of course, finally involve the study of the whole of Christian doctrine : but for our present practical purpose a less comprehensive inquiry will suffice. I have therefore selected the passages with which this study is prefaced, not to consider the specific teaching of each passage, but because they contain light which will help us.

D

Take the first of them, " Fear not, little flock ;
for it is your Father's good pleasure to give you
the Kingdom." These are the actual words of
Jesus. I am not dealing with the message of en-
couragement they contain, great and gracious as
it is and having some bearing on our subject of
prayer, as it has. I desire rather to look at the
verse from a purely literary standpoint, and in so
doing we find that Jesus recognizes all the
essential truth concerning God which He came to
reveal to man. Sometimes in ordinary conversa-
tion a very general statement will reveal the
speaker's whole philosophy on a certain subject.
When Jesus uttered these words He was not in-
tending to make a revelation of the Father, but
His conception of God flashes forth in great
clearness and beauty. If such a statement ap-
peared in a press issue from the pen of a modern
author, a merely literary critic might be tempted
to find a great deal of fault with it. I can imagine him saying, " Our author has fallen into a
strange mixture of metaphors. He begins, ' Fear
not, little flock,' and the figure in his mind is
evidently that of the shepherd and his sheep ;
but forgetting this, he continues, ' it is your
Father's good pleasure,' showing that he has
already mixed the figure of the shepherd and the
sheep with that of the father and the family ; and
again immediately he seems to have forgotten the
previous figures as he continues ' to give you the
Kingdom.' " We know perfectly that the metaphors of Jesus never clash. In this saying there

is a perfect unfolding of all the truth concerning
God which Jesus came to teach man. He is revealed as the Shepherd, Father, King. The
picture suggested is purely Eastern, and there can
be no doubt that in many respects, Eastern conditions explain fundamental positions far more
clearly than many of our Western methods do.
In the Arab tribe the Sheik is at once shepherd
of the flock, father of the family and king of the
nation. In those figures as Jesus used them He
takes us back to the original ideal of government.
Through the picture of the ancient economy He
reveals the eternal verities of which the material
things are but the shadow upon time's surface.
We must remember that these words were spoken
to His own. When He addresses those outside
He calls them first to submission to the Kingship
of God. No man ever found God as Father until
He recognized Him as King. In speaking to His
own the Master begins with the thought of the
Shepherd, then passes to that of the Father, and
finally to that of the King. At the heart of the
revelation is the thought of the Fatherhood. We
shall see that more clearly when we come to deal
with the pattern prayer, the whole of which is
addressed to the Father, the first half asking for
the setting up of the Kingdom, and the last for
the care and provision of the Shepherd. None of
these things were new. There is nothing in the
Gospels which had not been said in the Scriptures
of the old economy. Yet everything He said was
new. Men had said, " The Lord is my Shep-

herd" for ages, but when He said "I am the
good Shepherd" men understood as they had
never done before. In the midst of trouble, men
had constantly sung "Like as a father pitieth his
children, so the Lord pitieth them that fear
Him," but when Jesus said "Your Father knoweth," He revealed the meaning of Fatherhood far
more perfectly than the song which spoke of His
pity merely. Men had recognized Jehovah as
King, but Jesus came to reveal the meaning of
His Kingship. Nothing was new. Everything
was new. The old things blossomed into new
beauty such as humanity had never dreamed of.

It is only in proportion as we answer the
claims of this revelation that we are prepared for
prayer. As we are loyal to the King, like unto
the Father, content with the provision of the
Shepherd, we are ready to pray. All this is
surely self-evident. How can we pray "Thy
Kingdom come," if we are rebelling against the
King? How is it that our prayer so often fails
to prevail? Because we persist in praying, quite
honestly, "Thy Kingdom come" and yet in our
own heart we are not submissive to the King.
Something in the life is permitted which is contrary to His will; something in the business, the
friendships, the amusements. It is a solemn, yet
awful truth that we blaspheme when we pray for
the Kingdom to come and will not permit it to
obtain in our own life. It is an infinitely worse
thing that I should pray for God's Kingdom to
come in the world while I refuse to allow it to be

set up in my heart, than it is to take His name in
vain because I was born in a slum and had never
learned to revere it. If prayer is not prevailing in
our experience it is not because some scientific
teacher has denied its possibility, but rather because we are not responding to the revelation.
Of the significance of the Shepherd I would speak
in all tenderness. It is when I am resting in my
Shepherd's provision that I am able to pray. If
I am rebellious against my lot and persist in look-
ing upon my work as drudgery, I cannot pray.
It is the heart at leisure from itself because perfectly content with the Shepherd's provision,
that is able to pray. If I can truly say that
where'er my Shepherd leads I am content because He leads ; if through the desert, I am glad,
for that is best if 'tis His Will ; or if He leads by
waters still, I sing, not because the waters are
still and the pastures green, but because He
leads ; then I am able to pray. I pray God to
teach me that.

Jesus revealed God as Father. This fact is
central and final. How do we respond to it ? A
child responds to fatherhood when it reproduces
the father's likeness. That is something infinitely
beyond loyalty to Kingship, or content with pas-
ture. The child inherits his father's nature. If
I am a child of God I inherit my Father's nature.
The proportion in which I yield myself thereto
until it manifests itself through me is the measure of my power to pray. One illustration must
suffice. How can we hope to pray so as to pre-

vail while we call ourselves children of God, and yet nurse in our hearts bitterness and malice which are unlike God ? It is only when God's nature of love rules and reigns and inspires all our life, that we shall want to pray, and that our praying will prevail. To use the terminology of the praying man, is not to pray. To have the revelation and to answer it in loyalty to the King, in contentment with the provision of the Shepherd, in the reproduction of the Father's likeness, that is to pray.

Take a step further and consider the response of the soul to the fact of Christ's mediation. In his letter to the Corinthian Christians Paul had been contrasting the wisdom of men's words with the wisdom of the Word of the Cross. Assuring them that our Gospel, while a message of foolishness to the Greeks is not devoid of wisdom, in a comprehensive statement he declares what that wisdom is, " Of Him are ye in Christ Jesus, who was made unto us wisdom from God, and righteousness, and sanctification and redemption." Whether wisdom, righteousness, sanctification and redemption are separate and differing aspects of our Lord's work in the believer, or whether righteousness, sanctification and redemption are but the apostle's analysis of wisdom, the one all-inclusive word, appears to me immaterial, though personally I hold the latter interpretation. Christ is wisdom, and this wisdom of God is manifest in righteousness, sanctification and redemption. These three words cover the whole

fact of Christ's mediatorial work. They reveal
the tenses of the Christian life. These tenses are
indicated by three great words, righteousness,
sanctification, redemption. The past tense of
salvation is that experience to which I look back.
When I believed Christ was imputed to me as
righteousness. That was the salvation of my
spirit. The present tense of salvation is that
process through which I am now passing. Christ
is being imparted to me as sanctification. That
is the salvation of my mind. The future tense
of salvation is the life which is nearer than when
I believed. Christ will be implanted in me as
redemption. That is the salvation of my body.
The word translated redemption is always used
with regard to the coming glory. The same
word occurs in the letter to the Romans, " Even
we ourselves groan within ourselves, waiting for
our adoption, to wit, the redemption of our
body." Of course, it will be understood that I
do not mean that the English word redemption is
always used of the coming glory, but that the
Greek word so translated is always used in this
sense. It is most important that we should grasp
this threefold idea of our salvation. It consists
in Christ imputed as righteousness, imparted as
sanctification, implanted as glorification. I was
saved in the essential fact of my being, my spirit,
when in answer to my faith Christ was imputed
to me as the righteousness of God. I am being
saved in mind or consciousness as Christ through
all the discipline of the present life is being im-

parted to me as sanctification. I shall be saved finally when my body shall be fashioned anew in the likeness of His glorious beauty, when Christ shall be implanted within me and manifest through me. Through the mediatorial work of Jesus righteousness is made mine, sanctification is being made mine, redemption in its perfection will yet be made mine.

If we are to pray we must answer the claims of these truths. How am I to answer the claims of righteousness ? By yielding myself to God as one alive from the dead. In proportion as I do that I am prepared for prayer. The dynamic of prayer is holiness, which is rectitude of character, and righteousness, which is rectitude of conduct. Rectitude of conduct can only grow out of rectitude of character. Rectitude of character is given to me potentially when Christ is imputed to me. My responsibility is that I yield myself as one alive from the dead to Jesus Christ for righteousness. How am I to respond to sanctification ? Sanctification is the imparting of Christ to me, grace for grace. That is to say, every grace which is in Him, is in Him for me, and my responsibility is that I appropriate day by day what He communicates in order that He may reproduce Himself in me. When in order that I may be more perfectly conformed to His image, the indwelling Christ calls me to some new duty, some new sacrifice, some new enterprise, I must answer with ready consent. If I do, prayer prevails. If I refuse, prayer becomes impossible.

Finally, what response can I make to-day to the future tense of my life in Christ? Dr. James Denney in his book on Thessalonians says, "The attitude of expectation is the bloom, as it were, of the Christian character. Without it there is something lacking. The Christian who does not look onward and upward wants one mark of perfection. This is in all probability the point on which we should find ourselves most from home in the atmosphere of the Christian Church. Not unbelievers only, but disciples as well, have practically ceased to think of the second advent. . . . Yet a truth so clearly a part of Scripture teaching cannot be neglected without loss." I believe that to be most important truth. We have been so afraid of being called other-worldly, that we have not cared even to sing hymns about heaven. It is a grave mistake. We have been so afraid that some one would name us star-gazers, that we have abandoned all speech concerning the second advent. Yet the only light that we can ever shed upon the dark-ness of the world must be light beaming from the face lifted towards God's to-morrow. In the matter of prayer this is of supreme importance. To pray with prevailing power there must be the vision of the morning breaking in the Eastern sky. It is the man who sees the coming glory who knows what it is to put blood and sacrifice into the business of establishing that Kingdom here. In order to pray prevailingly, I must live in the power of the hope that maketh not ashamed, having my face ever lifted towards the light while I yet look at the sorrow around me, and serve diligently the will of my King.

Once again, there must be response to the Spirit. I am not now proposing to deal with the whole of the Spirit's work, but with that whereby He creates intercession. I would suggest three words as helpful in following the line of thought. They are, interpretation, consciousness, desire. The Spirit of God indwelling interprets. His interpretation creates a consciousness. That consciousness creates a desire, and that is prayer.

> Prayer is the soul's sincere desire
> Uttered or unexpressed ;
> The motion of a hidden fire
> That trembles in the breast.

The indwelling Spirit knows the will of God and interprets it to the soul in whom He abides. This He does by unveiling Christ, who is the revelation of the will of God to me. As He was the Word of God incarnate, He was the will of God incarnate. I come to Him that I may see what is God's will for myself and for all men ; that I may understand what is God's purpose concerning the whole world. As we look out upon the movements of the hour and upon all the facts of life, the indwelling Spirit sets them in relation to the will of God, and a keen consciousness is born within us of the failure in the midst of which we live. Thus the Spirit makes intercession in us with groaning which cannot be

uttered as He gives us this new consciousness of
the limitation and paralysis of all life without
God.   As the Spirit interprets to us the will of
God, He shows the disaster of being out of
harmony with that will.   As the Spirit interprets
the will of God, therefore, He makes the soul
profoundly discontented with everything that is
contrary thereto, and this because of the soul's
supreme content with the good and perfect and
acceptable will of God.   That is what the apostle
meant when he wrote, "The whole creation
groaneth and travaileth in pain together until
now.   And not only so, but ourselves also, which
have the first-fruits of the Spirit, even we ourselves groan within ourselves."   Faber sang this
sublime and overwhelming truth in simplest
words, "Earth's sorrows are most keenly felt in
heaven."   The heavenly people are, therefore,
those who most acutely feel earth's sorrows and
are able to enter into fellowship with God in
prayer for the winning of the victories of His
love.   Following consciousness of discontent is
that of desire for the coming of the Kingdom, for
the setting up of the will of God, which means
the healing of wounds and the breaking of chains.

To that work of the indwelling Spirit there
must be ready response.   "Quench not the Spirit."
When the Spirit interprets the will of God for
life, for home, for city, for nation, we must listen
to no other philosophy, be seduced by no other
ideal.   As the glories of that Kingdom flame
and flash before us, we must never be turned

aside by the glamour of the things of the world, the flesh and the devil. Answer the Spirit. Let Him teach. Let Him show the vision. Believe the Spirit. "Quench not the Spirit."

But more, infinitely more. When the Spirit revealing the will of God for the world creates in the heart a great pain and a great discontent, do not let us check it. That is what Christian men and women, alas, are too constantly doing. When the story of the sin and sorrow of humanity is told, they close their ears and are not willing to share in the pain. That is to grieve the Spirit indeed. We ought to hear. We ought to know. We ought to be ready to bring the new sensitiveness of our Christian life into close touch with the world's agony until we feel its pain as our very own. The Spirit desires that we should know its sorrow. His work is to interpret to us the meaning of the sob and sigh and the agony of the world. When we feel that, there will spring out of our life a new desire which will drive us to prayer that God's Kingdom may come, and to self-sacrificing service without which such prayer is blasphemy. Thus we shall begin to sob with God and to God, in our sense of the world's sorrow. Out of such prayer the toil and travail come which bring the Kingdom in.

Thus it will be seen that preparation for prayer is no slight, spasmodic process. It is the supreme matter of life. Yet, thank God, we can, if we will, respond to this revelation, mediation and inspiration so as to pray with prevailing power.

THE PLANE OF PRAYER
(a) The Purpose of God

" Our Father which art in heaven, Hallowed be Thy name. Thy Kingdom come. Thy will be done, as in heaven, so on earth."—MATTHEW 6 : 9, 10.

V

THE PLANE OF PRAYER
(a) The Purpose of God

WE now come to the consideration of the plane upon which prayer is operative, the subjects concerning which we have authority to pray. This plane is revealed in the pattern prayer as it occurs in the Manifesto of the King.

Some few preliminary words are necessary. I find there are some who object to the use of this prayer by Christian people. I have for a long time been endeavoring quite honestly to understand the position of such, and I think the objections which they raise may be briefly stated. First, there are those who do not use this prayer because they say its petition for forgiveness is not the Christian petition. They affirm that we have no need now to ask for the forgiveness of our debts on the basis of having forgiven our debtors. My answer to such is that they certainly do not understand the real meaning of this prayer, or else they do not understand themselves. Their objection, however, will best be dealt with when we come to the more particular consideration of that petition in the second part of the prayer. Others do not use the prayer because they declare they have no sins to confess or ask forgiveness for. Again, I can only say all such either do not understand the meaning of the words "debts" and "debtors," or else they are wofully self-deceived.   Perhaps the most serious and intelligent objection is that of those who say that this prayer was part of the Messianic Manifesto, that it had to do with Christ's teaching regarding the Kingdom, and that therefore it is the prayer of the Kingdom and not the prayer of the Church.   I carefully distinguished between the Kingdom of God, the Kingdom of heaven, and the Church of Jesus Christ, but I do not propose to discuss these distinctions now.   I recognize that the Church is, according to New Testament teaching, a separate entity having as its final purpose a vocation in the ages to come in the heavenly places.   While that is perfectly true and should never be forgotten, indeed must not be forgotten, it is also true that for the present hour all the principles of the Kingdom are committed to the Church to be realized within the Church and through the Church manifested to the world.   Consequently everything that Jesus said in His Manifesto concerning the Kingdom does apply to the Church.   As a matter of fact that Manifesto of the King does not apply at all to the outside world.   For the present day its only application is to the Church.   That is another point which I do not propose now to elaborate.   It is sufficient for the present purpose to say that to attempt to bring about the conditions described in the great Manifesto of the King among the vast unregenerate masses of the people is inevitably to be

doomed to disappointment. The things which
Jesus said to His disciples, I maintain, are only
applicable to those who are in His Kingdom and
subject to His rule. That Manifesto was the
enunciation of the ethic of the Kingdom which
no man can accept or obey while he is still in re-
bellion against the King Himself. That is a
broad and hurried statement; but if it be ac-
cepted it will be seen that in the Church which
for this age, according to the purpose of Jesus,
embodies the principles of the Kingdom and
manifests them in the world this prayer has its
rightful place. The supreme answer to objections to its use will be found in an understanding
of the prayer itself. In proportion as we really
comprehend its intention, its spaciousness, its
magnificence we shall be compelled to use it.
There can be no escape from the use of it for
such as are submitted to the reign and Lordship
of Jesus Christ and are in sympathy with Him
in His desires for the world.

Yet another word by way of introduction. It
has been affirmed and correctly so, that this is
not a new prayer. Its every petition is to be
found in the Talmudic writings. We are not
familiar with these writings, and so the different
petitions of the prayer are known to us only
through the Christian use of them. There can
be little doubt, however, that the men who
heard the Master when He first gave them the
prayer were familiar with all its petitions. In all
probability they had used them constantly in

their worship from childhood up. Now, while
that is true, it is also true that the prayer was
absolutely new as it came from the lips of Jesus.
He gathered together the things with which they
were most familiar and placed them in such perfect relation to each other as to reveal as never
before the whole plane of prayer. To pray that
prayer intelligently is to have nothing else to
pray for. It may be broken up, each petition
may be taken separately and expressed in other
ways, but in itself it is inclusive and exhaustive.
The Jewish Rabbis taught the people what were
known as "index prayers." These consisted of a
collection of brief sentences, each one of which
suggested a subject of prayer. One of their
habits of praying was to take such an index
prayer, recite one petition at a time, and elaborate it in the presence of God by carrying out its
thought; and endeavouring to express its full in-
tent. In that sense the Lord's prayer also is an
"index prayer." There can be no desire of the
human heart which is inspired of the Holy Spirit,
no petition presented to the throne of the Father
but that it is included in this prayer. The King
wove together all the essential petitions which lay
scattered over the field of human praying into
one perfect whole which covers the ground and
reveals to men for evermore the plane upon
which they may pray. Thus it is a pattern
prayer.

Turning to examination I shall ask you first of
all to notice its structure. I am so increasingly

convinced of the value of eye-gate that I want
you to look at the prayer in this form —

> Our Father which art in the heavens,
>   Thy name be hallowed,
>   Thy Kingdom come,
>   Thy will be done
>   as in heaven so on earth.
>   Give us this day our daily bread.
>   And
>   Forgive us our debts as we also have
>   forgiven our debtors.
>   And
>   Lead us not into temptation, but deliver us
>   from evil.

You will notice first that the doxology with
which the prayer closes is omitted. I suppose
most of us felt some kind of a pang when, taking
up the Revised Version, we found it absent. Yet
there can be no question as to the accuracy of the
omission. Even so conservative and scholarly an
expositor as Hengstenberg says concerning this
doxology that there is no doubt that it ought to
be omitted. He goes on to say that so perfect an
ending to the prayer had better be retained and
made perpetual use of. I have great sympathy
with the sentiment of that view, but it cannot be
permitted in any strict dealing with the Scripture. Personally I should never think of using
the prayer without the doxology, but I should
ever remember that the doxology was the answer
of man to the inspired prayer rather than a part
thereof. Now let us notice the structure of the
prayer as I have attempted to set it out. The
whole is introduced by an invocation —

Our Father which art in the heavens.

This invocation prepares the way not for the first three petitions only, but for the whole prayer. It is a reverent form of address, and by the use of it we are brought into the presence of the revealed Father.

Beyond the invocation the prayer falls into two parts. The first consists of three petitions with a qualifying phrase; the second consists of three petitions.

Let us look at the first three petitions, and the relation to them of the qualifying phrase.

> Thy name be hallowed,
> Thy Kingdom come,
> Thy will be done
>   as in heaven so on earth.

It is not "Thy will be done on earth as it is in heaven." The final phrase refers to all the petitions, and not merely to the last. The first half of the prayer is therefore one in which we ask that God's name may be hallowed, that His Kingdom may come, that His will may be done on this earth as in heaven. The three petitions form one whole petition. They mark stages in development. The first stage is the hallowing of the Name. That is followed necessarily by the crowning of the King and the coming of the Kingdom. When the King is crowned and the Kingdom established it is demonstrated amongst men by the doing of the will of the King by those who have hallowed His Name, and in whom the Kingdom

is established. Thus the first half of the prayer
has to do wholly with the purposes of God for
the world. In some senses all my need is included in this first half. It is not expressed there.
The only thing expressed is the passion for the
gaining of God's victory.

In the second half we have again three petitions —

> Give us this day our daily bread.
>   And
> Forgive us our debts, as we also
>   have forgiven our debtors.
>   And
> Bring us not into temptation, but
>   deliver us from evil.

Notice the position of the "and" in this setting,
how it links the second petition with the first, and
the third with the second. Notice also carefully
that the phrase "Bring us not into temptation,
but deliver us from evil," is not two petitions but
one. We are constantly hearing of the seven petitions of the Lord's prayer. There are only six,
and to make two petitions of the sixth is to create
difficulties which cannot be explained. Taken as
one it is a perfect petition, expressive at once of
the soul's caution and the soul's courage.

These last three petitions have to do wholly
with human and temporal needs as the three first
have to do with the Divine and eternal interests.
We shall not pray these last three petitions when
we get to heaven. I think the saints there are
still praying the first three. I think, moreover,
that they will continue to pray them until the

work is perfected, and that is not yet. Before
turning to fuller consideration of the first half of
this wonderful prayer, it is important to notice
that in its very structure there is teaching. Jesus
said, "Seek ye first His Kingdom, and His righteousness; and all these things shall be added unto
you." That was His order for life. It is also
His order for prayer. Prayer only fulfills the
Master's ideal when it begins with the interests
of God and follows with the needs of man. I am
afraid that order rebukes very much of our praying. Are we not all more or less in danger of
praying first for all our own needs, and then in a
closing sentence or two for the coming of the
Kingdom of God? Christ in the form of this
prayer teaches us that our first business in prayer
is to seek with God for His victory in the world;
that the deepest purpose of prayer is not that we
may obtain what we need, but that God should
gain that which glorifies His name. Passion for
the establishment of the Kingdom of God in the
world is the deepest note in prayer.

Now let us take the first part of the prayer and
look at it a little more closely. We find that the
word "heaven" occurs both in the invocation and
in the qualifying phrase. Its recurrence arrests
our attention, and at once we are conscious of a
light and glory irradiating these first petitions.
We pause therefore to inquire what this word is
and what it suggests. We shall find that it is
used in the New Testament with reference to
three distinct spheres, or places, or regions, which-

THE PLANE OF PRAYER

ever word may define most accurately the inde-
finable spaces beyond our earth. It is used first
of the atmosphere. "Behold the birds of the
heaven." It is also used of the stellar spaces
stretching far beyond the atmosphere. "I will
show wonders in the heavens." It is used of still
another region, of the dwelling place of other
beings, of the place where the glory of the infinite God is supremely manifest. "I knew a
man in Christ, fourteen years ago (whether in the
body, I know not; or whether out of the body, I
know not; God knoweth), such a one caught up
even to the third heaven." We cannot place
these ideas in relation to space because we know
so little concerning it. There is a sense in which
the third heaven enwraps and permeates the second and the first. All I want now to make clear
is that the word "heaven" is used with a threefold significance, and while poets and dreamers
speak of a "seventh heaven," the Bible speaks
only of a third. The word "heaven" therefore
stands for the atmosphere, the stellar spaces, and
finally the dwelling place of saints and angels.

Yet another note upon this word. It is written
sometimes in the singular and sometimes in the
plural and our translations do not show the difference uniformly. When in the singular it refers
to one or other of these heavens; when in the
plural it may refer to two or even three. The
context or evident sense of the passage must decide which of three. "The day of the Lord will
come as a thief; in the which the heavens shall

pass away with a great noise." The reference
here is evidently to the atmospheric and the stellar
spaces, the two first heavens. Stephen when dying exclaimed, "Behold, I see the heavens opened,
and the Son of Man standing on the right hand
of God." He saw beyond the atmosphere, and
beyond the stellar spaces into that place where
God's glory is supremely manifest and the spirits
of just men are.

In the invocation the word "heaven" is plural.
In the qualifying phrase at the close of the first
three petitions it is singular. "Our Father which
art in the heavens." Which of them? All of
them. Thus there is found at the portal of the
prayer the doctrine of the transcendence and im-
manence of God. Your thought cannot carry you
so far away as to escape Him; and yet where you
are at this moment, "Closer is He than breathing,
and nearer than hands and feet." Let us try to
realize this by the simplest of simple diagrams.

SAINTS AND SERAPHIM

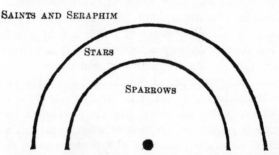

STARS

SPARROWS

Taking that dot as centre I sweep a segment of
a circle round it to represent the atmosphere

which extends for forty miles outward from the
earth. That is the first heaven of the New Testament. Beyond that I sweep a larger segment
representing the vast stellar spaces. That is the
second heaven. Beyond that again is the third
heaven. In the first circle I write the word "sparrows"; in the next "stars," and in the next "saints
and seraphim." We are here on this little earth,
and having seen the revelation of the Father and
yielded to the mediation of the Son, and answered
the inspiration of the Spirit we are prepared for
prayer. Jesus now says to us, "After this manner therefore pray ye; Our Father which art in
the heavens." That is to say that the God who
hears prayer is in all the heavens. That great and
gracious fact is proven by other words of the Divine oracles. He is in the first heaven, the atmosphere; "Are not two sparrows sold for a
farthing? and not one of them shall fall on the
ground without your Father." Let us most ear-
nestly guard against spoiling the thought in that
quotation by adding to it a single word. It is
constantly rendered, " not one of them shall fall
on the ground without your Father's *knowledge*."
Jesus did not say that. It would have been a
beautiful thing to say, but what He said was finer
far, "not one of them shall fall on the ground
without your Father." He not only watches from
afar the sparrow's fall, but He holds it dying.
The frailest bird dying of summer heat or winter
cold is not alone. It dies in the company of God.
And what of the stars of the second heaven?

"By the greatness of His might, and for that He is strong in power, not one is lacking." "Upholding all things by the word of His power." And what of the saints and seraphim? They veil their faces in the presence of His glory, and do His will in the consciousness of His nearness.

Thus as I begin to pray according to the pattern which the Lord gives me, I find at the portal of my prayer a doctrine of God which assures me that nothing is beyond His reach, and nothing is too small for His presence and attention. Oh, the infinite comfort of it! Mother, praying for your boy at the other side of the world, think of it! Your Father is with him there. He is as near to him as He is to you. Jesus did not say, Our Father who is away off in some distant heaven far removed from us; but rather, Our Father who art in all the heavens; close at hand so that the least whisper reaches Him, far away so that nothing can escape Him.

Coming to the phrase with which these petitions end we find that the word "heaven" is singular. Now, while I do not mean to suggest that God's will is not done in the atmosphere or in the stellar spaces, I think it is evident that Christ's use of the singular at this point indicates the fact that His special reference was to that heaven where God's glorious presence is supremely manifest, and where the one abiding law is the law of His will. Thus when we pray this prayer we are asking that as His name is hallowed by the saints and seraphim, as His Kingdom is established among them, and

as His will is the one and only law of all their activity, so on this earth His name may be hallowed,
His Kingdom come, and His will be done. It is a
prayer that the order of heaven may be established
on earth. When Jesus uttered these words and
gave them to His disciples as a pattern of prayer,
He of course knew perfectly that order of the third
heaven. Indeed His vision and perfect knowledge
of that heavenly order were the inspiration of His
desire as He stood among the sin and sorrow of
this world. As we interpret the prayer through
the One who gave it to us, it becomes an inspiration making us desire to know the order of the
third heaven. Can we know anything of that
order other than speculatively? If there is one
thing concerning which no man ever ought to
speculate, it is heaven. We have suffered terribly
in our ideas of heaven from grotesque imagination
concerning it. I remember as boy that heaven
was to me a place where the saints sat on thrones
forever and ever wearing white robes and having
harps in their hands. It was suggestive of deadly
monotony and far from attractive. Such is not
the meaning of heaven. Jesus did not want us to
pray that an order of that kind should be set up
on earth. He was Himself a revelation to man
of the heavenly order. Of the four evangelists
John is the one who interprets to us most perfectly
Christ as the Word of God out of heaven. The
word "heaven" in John's Gospel is never plural,
and it always has reference to the third heaven.
The key words of John's writings are love, light,

life. " God is love," " God is light," " God is life."
These are three of the simplest words, and yet in
all human speech there are none sublimer. These
words perfectly portray the order obtaining in the
heaven of God. Grant me these three words with
all they suggest, and I care nothing about robes
and harps and thrones. There may be all these
things and will be, only do not let us forget that
all that we know of earth's beauties and splen-
dours are not worthy to be compared with the
grace and glory yet to be revealed.

In the third heaven love is the satisfactory impulse of everything. Light is the perfect intelligence in which all the inhabitants act. Life is
the sufficient power by which they walk in light
answering love. Love is impulse. Light is intelligence. Life is energy. The contrast between
the order of the third heaven and that obtaining
on earth to-day is at once manifest. No one is
prepared to affirm that love is the final reason of
all the activity of the world to-day. Christ says,
Pray that it may become so. Men do not walk
in perfect light even when it flashes upon their
pathway, for, as in the days of Christ so still,
men love darkness rather than light, for their
works are evil. Christ says, " Pray that men
may come to love light, and walk in it." And
yet men have not life sufficient to do the highest
and the best even when they know it. Toiler for
God, in your specific service you know what it is
to be weary. Do you know what weariness is ?
It is the touch of death. Press your toil a little

further, a little too far, and all the weary wheels
stand still, and your eye sees no light, and your
heart can no longer love. That is the condition
of man in the world to-day. In God's third
heaven everything is different. Love is the reason of devotion and worship. Love is the inspiration of giving and receiving. Love is the impulse of revelation and explanation. Every move-
ment of the wing of the cherubim and every
note of the song of the seraphim are alike love-
impulsed. In heaven when love impulses light
falls upon the pathway, and mistakes are never
made through ignorance. There as in answer to
love the inhabitants serve in perfect light; they
are never weary for theirs is endless life. Jesus
said, Pray that all this may be so also on this
earth. Think what it would mean, what it will
mean for the world when that prayer is answered,
when "love" is the only reason, and "light" is
perfect intelligence, and "life" is sufficient power
for all accomplishment.

Can that prayer be answered? Will it be answered? The first reply to such a question is
that Jesus never taught men to utter vain prayers.
The fact that He gave us this prayer is enough
to make us offer it in the midst of the world's sin
and sorrow and sighing, knowing that because He
taught us so to pray the answer is bound to come.
And yet there is another and profounder argument for the reasonableness of this prayer, and
that is Christ Himself. Once in the history of
the world that for which the prayer asks has been

perfectly realized. Once the world saw, though
it did not understand it, the heavenly order. It
was manifest when He, who taught us to pray,
tabernacled amongst men. Studying the life of
Jesus as we have it in the fourfold Gospel, it is
perfectly evident that wherever and whenever we
find Him the one reason of His being, or doing,
or saying anything is love. He was perfectly
and wholly impulsed by love. This is true not
only of His words and acts most evidently tender, but also of the severe things He said and
did. Some of these were terrible indeed, scorching and startling men. On one occasion He
looked into the faces of the rulers of His people
and said, "Woe unto you, Scribes and Pharisees,
hypocrites"; and it is impossible to read these
words without being conscious that there was a
note of terror in the voice of Jesus when He
cried "Woe." Was that love? Yes, let Him
finish His sentence, "for ye devour widows'
houses." Love for the oppressed creates anger
with the oppressor for evermore. Is there any
phrase more startling than "the wrath of the
Lamb"? I think that if we had desired to de-
scribe wrath figuratively we should have written,
the wrath of the "lion," but therein we should
have failed. It is the wrath of the Lamb which
is terrible, the wrath of One whose very heart
and nature are love and gentleness. Wrath kin-
dled by love is the fiercest flame that burns.

It is also true that in all the life of Jesus there
was manifest the light of a perfectly informed

intelligence. He never hesitated. He was never
perplexed. He never took counsel even with His
own disciples. He consulted neither Conventions,
Conferences, nor Committees. Ah, some one ac-
quainted with the New Testament challenges that
statement, and suggests that at least upon one
occasion He called His disciples into Consultation.
There was a day on which He asked one of them
what was to be done to feed the multitude : but
continue the story and you will read " *This He
said to prove him :* for He Himself knew what
He would do."   Thus on the only occasion when
it is ever suggested that He took counsel with His
disciples the evangelist is careful to tell us that it
was not that He might get advice, but in order
that He might teach them something. He ever
passed straight onward, and that perpetually on
an illuminated pathway. Answering love He
saw His way before Him and without hesitation
walked in it.

But, it will be said it was not true of Him that
He had endless life—He died. Let me say first
in answer to such an objection, that the life of
Jesus was always sufficient for the doing of the
will of God, and even though He knew in sympathy with us the heavy weariness which follows
toil, He was never weary while God-appointed
service waited for Him. And yet again, He had
the power of endless life as witness His own
strange words, " I lay down My life, that I may
take it again. No one taketh it away from Me,
but I lay it down of Myself. I have power to lay

it down, and I have power to take it again. This
commandment received I from My Father."
Death in the case of every other man is a fact
from which He cannot escape. Death in the case
of Jesus was an act in the mystery of which He
was yet the supreme Lord and Master. He died
and rose again in fulfillment of these wonderful
words. Once in human history the heavenly
order has been seen in a Man who answered love
and walked in light, and had such life as enabled
Him to die and to live again, and so doing to fling
up a highway out of death for all such as trust
and follow Him.

But what did the world do with this Revealer?
The story is that of the world's final tragedy.
Hatred murdered love. Darkness put out light.
Death conquered life.

The Cross was man's answer to this prayer.
But again, the Cross was God's answer to this
prayer. Put both things together, or let us hear
them put together by Peter in the first message
delivered after Pentecost. "Him, being delivered
up by the determinate counsel and foreknowledge
of God, ye by the hand of lawless men did crucify
and slay." Man's attitude towards the revelation
of the heavenly order—" ye by the hand of lawless men did crucify and slay," God's activity in
the midst of the mystery of death—" delivered up
by the determinate counsel and foreknowledge of
God." Over against the lawlessness of man's
murder the deliberate counsel of God is operative,
and thus the very Cross which marks man's re-

fusal of the Kingdom becomes the means by which that Kingdom is yet to be set up.

When thus we observe the Man who taught us this prayer and come to understand that He embodied in His own life the principles He bids us seek, and when we know that by His Cross He made it possible for every man to come after Him, to answer "love," and to walk in " light " in the power of "life," then we pray the first part of this prayer as never before, realizing that in the name and merit and might of Him who taught us so to pray its final answer must come.

Thus the pattern prayer teaches us first that we must take the whole world into our praying, and that we must see clearly that the line of its redemption is that of return to conformity to the will of God, made possible by the life and death and resurrection of Him who taught us to pray—

> Our Father which art in the heavens,
>   Thy name be hallowed,
>   Thy Kingdom come,
>   Thy will be done,
>   as in heaven so on earth.
>   Give us this day our daily bread.
>   And
>   Forgive us our debts, as we also
>   have forgiven our debtors.
>   And
>   Lead us not into temptation,
>   but deliver us from evil.

THE PLANE OF PRAYER
(b) The Pilgrimage of Man

" Give us this day our daily bread.   And forgive us our debts, as we also have forgiven our debtors.   And bring us not into temptation, but deliver us from the evil one."—MATTHEW 6 : 11-13.

VI

THE PLANE OF PRAYER

(b) The Pilgrimage of Man

WE now come to the second part of the pattern prayer. As the first part has to do with the interests of God, the second half deals with the pilgrimage of man; that is to say, it has to do with the needs of man in the days of his sojourn in this world. Its three petitions express the needs of these days of pilgrimage towards the Father's home. It will be impossible to use these petitions when we reach that home. They express our present need in the listening ear of God.

If these petitions be intelligently apprehended, it will be found that they cover the whole of our possible requirements. We may break up the petitions, we may give expression in the hours of communion with God to the detailed and specific need of which we are conscious, but we cannot pray for anything which is not included in these requests.

In previous chapters we have dealt with the threefold fact concerning God which Jesus has revealed. He is King, Father, Shepherd. In that order men come into relationship with Him. Having submitted to His Kingship, they find Him to be their Father. Then as they begin to walk along the pathway which His will appoints, they experience His care as a Shepherd.

The part of the prayer at which we are now to look is the cry of children-subjects, asking for the privileges of the flock, for the care of the one great Shepherd. In it there are three petitions —

> Give us this day our daily bread.
> And
> Forgive us our debts, as we also
> have forgiven our debtors.
> And
> Bring us not into temptation, but deliver us
> from evil, or, from the evil one.

As we study these three petitions we shall find that in each of them three sets of forces with which we daily come in contact are recognized. Every man upon the pathway of his pilgrimage has to do every day with God, with man and with the devil. That fact may be expressed in other words. We may say that we have to do with the upper world, with the world about us, and with the under world of evil. Every day we who are children of God have necessarily some dealings with God; every day we are in contact with our fellow man; and I do not think any one will dispute with me when I declare that for the saint of God there is no day in which he or she has not something to do with the spirits of evil. The three worlds are present in every one of these petitions, but in each petition one realm is referred to with special em-

phasis.   To take the first, "Give us this day our
daily bread."   That petition has to do preeminently with our relationship to God, our de-
pendence upon Him; but we shall find recognized in it our relationship to our fellow man,
and also our relationship to the spirits of evil.
The preëminent note is our relationship to God.
In the second petition, "Forgive us our debts as
we also have forgiven our debtors," the principal
emphasis is upon our relationship to our fellow
men.   The relationship to God is acknowledged
and the relationship to the under world is evident.   In the final petition, "Lead us not into
temptation, but deliver us from evil," the principal
emphasis is upon our relationship to the under
world.   Our relationship to God is also recognized and that to our fellow man is present.

When referring to the threefold fact of the
heavenly order proceeding from the government
of God we mentioned three words which are
constantly repeated in the writings of John,
"Life," "Light," and "Love."   The first of these
three petitions is a cry for sustenance to God as
"Life."   The second is a cry for rectitude to God
as "Light."   The last is a cry for victory to God
as "Love."   So that the threefold order, which
we first are taught to pray may be established in
the world, is recognized when we continue to
pray about our own personal and individual
needs.

In the economy of Jesus Christ, prayer never
loses sight of the infinite relationships and the

infinite values. Herein is the test for our praying. The moment prayer becomes request for
something purely for self which may be spent
upon personal lusts—or if you will have a milder
word, upon personal desires—then prayer is outside the will of God. If I ask for sustenance it
must be in a petition which recognizes that real
life is related to the life of God. If I ask for
rectitude it must be in a petition which recognizes rectitude as being in right relationship with
the light of God. If I ask for succour, deliverance from the evil of the under world, it must be
in a petition which recognizes the tender love of
God manifesting itself supremely in its persistent
determination that I shall be delivered from evil.
So that all prayer is to be tested by its relationship to the infinite and eternal verities and values.

Let us now take the petitions one by one. In
the first, " Give us this day our daily bread," we
have the threefold relationship. First, it is a cry
to God as " Life " for sustenance. There is also
recognized the relationship to man. We cannot
begin to pray this prayer alone; we immediately
bring others with us into the place of prayer not
as to bodily presence but as to social interest.
That fact is true of the whole prayer, but specially
true of the first petition. We have also the reference to the under world, because life fed with
daily bread is made strong against the solicita-
tion of the spirits of evil. The principal emphasis is, however, upon our relation to God.
What then does this prayer mean, " Give us this

day our daily bread " ? What is daily bread ?
What did our Lord mean we were to pray for at
this point ? Let us omit the word " daily " for
the moment, and read " Give us this day our
bread." Of what bread was He speaking ?
There are those who hold that this prayer simply
has reference to the bread of the physical life,
and there are thousands of people who use it only
in that sense. There are other people, some of
them gifted expositors of the Word of God, who
hold that our Lord was not referring in any way
to the physical bread but that this is wholly a
spiritual prayer, and that therefore He is here referring to the sustenance of the spiritual life. I
do not agree with either of these interpretations.
I believe that when our Lord enjoins us to pray
" Give us this day our bread " He means by the
use of that word all that is necessary for the
sustenance of the whole life, physical and
spiritual. I believe that, because I never find
Jesus dealing with men in compartments. He
always dealt with the whole man, and when He
taught us to pray this prayer He intended to
teach us that we were perpetually to remember
that we are absolutely dependent upon God for
all that is necessary for the sustenance of our
perfect and complete life. In Deuteronomy we
read " Man doth not live by bread only, but by
everything that proceedeth out of the mouth of
the Lord." There, in these words He quoted in
the midst of His own temptation, is His own
recognition of the need of physical bread ; and

therein is His affirmation of the necessity for
another bread, the Word proceeding out of the
mouth of God. He Himself being the Word of
God said, " I am the bread of life." When this
petition is presented we are asking God to give
us the sustenance necessary for our whole life,
that necessary for our spiritual, and that necessary for our physical life. The latter is secondary
but it is necessary, and is as much supplied by
God as is the sustenance for the spiritual life.
The first petition of our need is one in which we
ask our Father to supply all that is necessary for
our complete sustenance " Give us this day our
bread."

I think that an understanding of the word
" daily " will emphasize the accuracy of the interpretation I have given. There is difficulty
here. As a matter of fact it is a word quite un-
known in classical Greek, and it is a word which
never occurs in the New Testament except at this
point in Matthew 6 and in Luke 11 where our
Lord took one or two petitions of the prayer and
gave them to His disciples in answer to their request. It would be a fascinating theme for discussion and speculation as to where this word
came from and what it really means. There are
difficulties in tracing its root. You notice in the
margin of the Revised Version this suggestion,
" Give us this day our bread ' for the coming
day.'" If you have noticed it, you have felt
how curious a suggestion it is. I want to speak
with all due carefulness, and I do not speak with-

out remembering that the marginal readings of
the Revised Version express the opinion of a majority of the translators. Nevertheless, I do not
think that the meaning of this word translated
"daily" is "the coming day." It is possible that
it came from a root which means "to-morrow";
but it is equally possible that it came from a root
implying "existence." It is not for me to go into
that particularly, but I do not hesitate to say my
own belief is that the latter is the root from
which this word "daily" came. "Give us this
day our bread of existence." Here is a piece of
speculation which you may accept or forget as
you like. I believe Jesus coined that word. You
cannot find it anywhere else. Then of course
there comes the question as to whether Jesus
spoke in Aramaic or Greek, and again we are face
to face with a question full of interest, and one
which I do not pretend to be able dogmatically
or finally to decide. Personally, I am of opinion
that the Gospel of Matthew was written in Greek,
and moreover that Jesus spoke a dialect of Greek
which was common at the time. It is interesting
to remember that Alford in his later editions
adopted that view, although in the earlier issues
of his work he had maintained the contrary. I
believe therefore that Jesus coined this word
"daily." What He told us to pray was, "Give
us to-day the bread we need for our existence";
that is, for our whole life, for the life which is
physical, for the life which is spiritual.

Passing from that discussion of the mere words

of the petition, let us think of its spiritual intention and meaning. We are to ask God every day
for what we need for the sustenance of our life.
There are two ways in which we neglect this petition. One way is that we pray it as though it
simply referred to the bread which feeds the body,
and forget that we need day by day to be fed by
God with the bread which supplies our spiritual
life. As God answers prayer for the bread of
the body so He answers prayer for the bread of
the spirit. How does God answer our prayer for
the bread of the body ? Not by its miraculous
supply but by the gift of all such forces as are
necessary to enable us in coöperation with Himself to obtain for ourselves by labour the bread
we need. So with the spiritual bread. God does
not succour the spiritual life of any man on his
simple asking. Our spiritual life can only be
maintained and sustained as we in personal labour for the meat that endureth, meditate in His
Word day and night, feeding upon that Bread of
Life which came down out of heaven from God.

The other side of the lesson is that we are not
to forget in these days of incipient infidelity in
the Christian Church, that the table to which we
sit down every day is one He spreads. You have
heard the old story of the man who met a boy
in a village street carrying a loaf of bread. He
stopped the boy and asked him where he got the
loaf. "From the baker" was the reply. "Yes,
that is right, but where did he get it ?" "He
made it," said the boy. "How did he make it ?"

"With flour." "Where did he get his flour?"
"He ground the corn." "Where did he get his
corn from?" "He got it from the farmer."
"Yes, but where did the farmer get his corn?"
"Oh, from God," said the boy. "Then you got
your loaf from God!" We have been very much
like that boy. We have put God away back, behind the miller and the farmer, and have forgotten Him in the process. While we recognize the
need of the intermediation of all these instru-
ments, we are not to forget that it is God who
feeds us with food sufficient for body and soul.

> Back of the loaf is the snowy flour,
> And back of the flour the mill;
> And back of the mill is the wheat, and the shower,
> And the sun, and the Father's will.

This prayer brings me back every day as a dependent being to God, so that I have never any
right to pray this prayer if I am saying in my life
or by my actions, my own hand gets me this bread,
my own cunning, wit and wisdom provide for me
all I need of spiritual culture.

Notice the social character of this prayer. Have
you ever taken the trouble to write out the personal pronouns in the first person? If you have,
you will have discovered that there is not one in
the singular from beginning to end,—our, us, our,
us, our, we, our, us, us. They are all plural.
You cannot pray that prayer by yourself. You
cannot pray that short petition by yourself. I
remember a friend of mine, a deacon in one of

my former churches, on a certain Harvest Festival, came to me in my vestry and said—there was a deal of humour in him, there always is in saintly men,—" Well, Pastor, I suppose you won't use the Lord's Prayer to-night. We are going to thank Him for having supplied our daily bread, you won't ask Him for it?" I replied that we should certainly use the Lord's Prayer that night, and that by so doing we should put ourselves into fellowship with all hungry souls. It is "us" and "our," not "me" and "mine." When we come into God's presence to ask for the supply of our own need we are to remember in loving sympathy the need of all those who have not yet received.

There is another suggestive fact about this prayer. There is only one nominative case in it. There are four objective and four possessive, but only one nominative. Do you not know that the nominative is the most popular case. Men like to talk in the first person singular, nominative ; but the nominative is only here once. "Forgive us our debts, as we also have forgiven our debtors." The only right in this prayer to be the subject of a sentence is that of the loving heart who forgives some other man. The prayer is a social prayer from beginning to end. The social quality is manifest in this first petition as it asks for sustenance not for " me and mine," but for " us and ours."

The relation to the under world is also recognized here. The man fed, physically and spiritually, is the man most likely to be strong against the solicitations of evil. That is why men are perfectly right when they tell us that we insult a hungry man when we offer him a tract about heaven. The first thing is to feed him, not simply because he clamours for bread, but because a fed man is one the devil does not like. It is the hungry man the devil attacks. If that be true physically, it is preeminently true spiritually. My brother see to it that when morning breaks you go to God for sustenance for your spiritual life. That will make you strong against the allurements of the devil. So many people turn out to face the temptations of the day spiritually unfed, spiritually hungry therefore, and they are attacked by all kinds of enticements of the enemy. It is the man fed by God, spiritually and physically who is likely to overcome in the hour of temptation.

In the second petition will you notice that the relation to God comes first. It always does even if the emphasis is not there. We are to ask forgiveness—this is the one petition to which most people object, and some attempt to escape from the prayer because of it. I am not particularly surprised that people criticise this petition more than any other. It is a very difficult one to pray, but let us remember that when Christ gave this prayer in His Manifesto, He commented only upon this petition. " For if ye forgive not men their trespasses, neither will your Father forgive your trespasses." So we must neither get away from this petition, nor indulge in that criticism which attempts to accommodate it to our own failure. I had been speaking on this subject in an American city, and afterwards received a letter from a lady who was greatly perturbed because I had put special emphasis upon the fact that Jesus distinctly tells us we are to ask for forgiveness when we have forgiven. She said that for years she had changed the form of that petition for she had been afraid of it, and had said, " Forgive us our debts, and we will forgive our debtors." She asked if I did not consider this to be sufficient. I replied that God never does business on the basis of a promissory note. We must get our forgiving done before we can ask for forgiveness. That prayer is the prayer of the children of God, not of the men outside. I do not go to the man outside who has never given himself to God and tell him that if he will forgive everybody, God will forgive him. God begins by forgiving us of His own free grace without any condition. The unforgiven man can be forgiven now, without any condition except that he believe on the Lord Jesus Christ. He will blot out the sins of such like a thick cloud. When that is done the soul enters the Kingdom, and now Jesus superimposes upon His own subject as the condition for forgiveness that he should be forgiving. If we are unforgiving, in the necessity of the case God will not forgive us. There is no escape from it. Is not hatred the most dastardly and heinous of all sins— hatred, the thing that contradicts the essence of

God which is love? If in my heart there is bitterness and malice and revengefulness what is the
use of confessing other sins and expecting to be forgiven, nursing the while the most damnable sin?
We who are children of God, subjects of the King,
flock of the Shepherd, cannot be forgiven unless
we forgive, for our refusal to forgive is the deepest
and worst sin of all. I speak with such emphasis
because I think the Church of Jesus Christ is
cursed by an unforgiving spirit. Men and women
are sitting down at the table of the Lord who do
not speak to each other. We are unforgiving in
our theological controversies. The sin for which
Moses was excluded from the earthly promised
land was that " He spake unadvisedly with his
lips," he manifested a provoked spirit in a righteous cause. A righteous cause, but an angry, unforgiving man; and God shut him out of the
land of earthly promise. For evermore Jesus
Christ is saying to us every day, "Come and have
your Father's forgiveness for trespasses, but do
not ask for that until you have forgiven the man
who has trespassed against you." What is trespass? For notice, in the actual text our Lord
used the words " Debt " and " debtors " and in
the exposition which follows, He used the word
" trespasses." What then is debt, trespass?
There is a common quality in our Master's use of
the two words which helps us to understand it.
Trespass is intentional error, or willful transgres-
sion. Trench has said the word means falling
where one should have stood upright, whether

G

one could help it or not. There of course arises the whole question of sin and of what sin is. We still believe that the whole meaning of the New Testament evangel is that a man need not sin willfully, but we still maintain that so long as we walk the pathway of the earthly pilgrimage, in comparison with God's high ideal we are as trespassers, coming short, so that of our best service we have to say "we are unprofitable servants."

I pity the man who tells me he cannot pray this prayer because he never trespasses. I pity him because of his dim comprehension of the real meaning of holiness and of sin. To the man who walks in light there is no day when he does not find it necessary to confess his trespasses. Let us not forget this flaming scorching word of the Master, that we are not to ask for forgiveness until we have forgiven. "If therefore thou art offering thy gift at the altar, and there rememberest that thy brother hath aught against thee, leave there thy gift before the altar, and go thy way, first be reconciled to thy brother and then come and offer thy gift." I wonder how many people would have to stay away from church next Sunday if they were true to this word. We had better stay away, and get right with our brother before we come to the altar. "If ye forgive not men their trespasses, neither will your Father forgive your trespasses." Loving forgiveness of my brother is the condition upon which I, a child of God, may ask His forgiveness.

What relation has all this to the underworld

of evil? When we forgive those who have
wronged us, we have gained the mightiest victory
possible over the devil. In that day when we
trampled on our pride and sacrificed what we
speak of as our rights, when we triumphed over
pride and lovingly forgave the man who had
sinned against us, we know we were conscious of
God as we had never been before, and we were
conscious of victory over the enemy as we had
never been. There is nothing God loves and the
devil hates more than a man who can forgive.

We come to the last of these petitions. "And
bring us not into temptation, but deliver us from
the evil one." "Bring us not into temptation,"
that is the language of the cautious heart, of the
man who recognizes how terrible an experience
temptation is. But there is something more important than that I should be delivered from
temptation, and that is that I should be delivered
from evil. If I can only be delivered from evil
by passing through temptation, then that I be
delivered from evil is the supreme matter. In
that remarkable passage in Luke just before the
Gethsemane experience and again just after it,
the Lord said to His disciples, "Pray that yĕ enter not into temptation." He was passing down
to temptation then. As I watch Him in Gethsemane I hear the echo of temptation, "Father,
if Thou be willing, remove this cup from Me;
nevertheless not My will, but Thine be done."
That is the echo of temptation. I have heard
that before. I heard the enemy say to Him long

ago in the wilderness, " There are the Kingdoms
of the world which you have come to possess.
Your pathway to them is one of suffering and
shame. Fall down and worship me and I will
give them to you. Get to your goal by a short
cut." Here is the old method. Be very afraid
of any easy method to anything. I hear it again
later on, not as before in the open attack of the
foe, but through the subtle word of friendship.
When Jesus at Cæsarea Philippi mentioned the
cross, Peter said, " Not that, Lord! That be far
from Thee. Keys, yes; crowning, yes; building, yes; but not the cross !" Christ said to him,
" Get thee behind Me, Satan : thou art a stumbling-
block unto Me; for thou mindest not the things
of God, but the things of men." In the garden
of Gethsemane the devil comes no longer in open
attack, no longer in the guise of a friend, but in
the shrinking of His own soul. "If Thou be
willing, remove this cup from Me." Therein is
the philosophy of this petition, " Bring us not
into temptation." We are to be afraid of temptation. We are not to be foolhardy, treating it
as of no account. We are to shrink in its presence with that cautiousness which makes for
courage. But the more important thing is that
we should be delivered perfectly from evil.
"Bring us not into temptation, but deliver us
from evil." That is to be my prayer every day
to God who governs in hell as well as in heaven.
Recognition of the force of temptation and its
subtlety will make me pray, " Bring me not into

temptation," but the deepest passion of my whole life will be—"deliver me from evil."

What relation to other men is suggested in this last petition? Peter writing to Christian people said, "Be sober, be watchful: your adversary the devil, as a roaring lion, walketh about, seeking whom he may devour." Why were they to be sober and watchful? "Knowing that the same sufferings are accomplished in your brethren who are in the world." Let the light of that fall upon this petition. When we are face to face with the evil one and with temptation, we are not fighting a lonely battle, we are part of a great host. Our brethren are being tried also. If we win, they win in a greater measure. If we lose, we shall halt the whole battle and retard the final victory. I sometimes think if we could say this to young people as it ought to be said we might help them. Are you fighting against temptation? Remember it is not a lonely battle you are fighting, you are part of a great host. If you lose, if you are beaten, if the enemy overcomes you, the whole army of God is halted in its onward march. If you win, you hasten the coming of the Kingdom. The same sufferings are being accomplished in your brethren. Upon this stress and strife of the saints depends the hastening or retarding of the Day of God. So we are to pray together "Bring us not into temptation, but deliver us from evil." We fear the process, but there is a deeper passion than the passion for escape from testing, it is the pas-

102 THE PRACTICE OF PRAYER

sion for deliverance from evil. That is the great
and final thing.

In conclusion, let it be noted that He who
taught the prayer has in its second half, as in the
first, guaranteed the answer. Am I to pray for
the bread of life ? He bends over me and says,
" I am the Bread of Life." Am I to pray for
sustenance of the physical life ? He whispers to
me, hear the tender promise, " All these things
shall be added unto you." Am I to pray for forgiveness ? Through His name is forgiveness
preached. But how am I going to forgive the
man who has injured me ? The Spirit of Jesus
is the spirit of forgiveness. If I am yielded to
Him He is yielded to me. If I give my whole
life to Him He will give His whole life to me.
If I have Jesus for my own I shall be able to forgive, so that He will answer this very prayer and
make possible its answer in the high court of
God's own judgment hall. As to temptation,
" He was tempted in all points like as we are, sin
apart." And " IN that He Himself hath suffered
being tempted, He is able to succour them that
are tempted."

So in this pattern prayer He shows me what to
pray for as He opens before my astonished vision
the whole realm of prayer. I end as I begin by
saying that if we can pray this prayer with spiritual intelligence and earnestness we pray all
prayer.

THE PRACTICE OF PRAYER

" *And when ye pray, ye shall not be as the hypocrites : for they love to stand and pray in the synagogues and in the corners of the streets, that they may be seen of men.   Verily I say unto you, They have their reward.   But thou, when thou prayest, enter into thine inner chamber, and having shut thy door, pray to thy Father which is in secret, and thy Father which seeth in secret shall recompense thee.   And in praying use not vain repetitions, as the Gentiles do ; for they think that they shall be heard for their much speaking. Be not therefore like unto them : for your Father knoweth what things ye have need of, before ye ask Him.*"—MATTHEW 6 : 5–8.*

" *Again I say unto you, that if two of you shall agree on earth as touching anything that they shall ask, it shall be done for them of My Father which is in heaven.   For where two or three are gathered together in My name, there am I in the midst of them.*"—MATTHEW 18 : 19, 20.*

VII

THE PRACTICE OF PRAYER

THE subjects already considered are all preliminary to and necessary for the present one. God has made prayer possible to us through Jesus. We can pray prevailingly only as we respond to the truths which create the possibility. The sphere of prayer includes the coming of the Kingdom of God and the provision of all the need of the saints. Thus all these constitute an integral part of the subject of the practice of prayer. Prayer is only possible to the revealed Father through the mediating Son by the inspiring Spirit. Prayer is only a prevailing power as, in the life, the child of God is loyal to His Kingship, satisfied with His provision, conformed to His likeness. Moreover, it can only be operative within the sphere revealed in the pattern prayer.

All this being granted, we now come to the more technical consideration of this subject. It is necessary both in order to brevity and clearness that we should follow a process of elimination. The teaching of Jesus is so full of instruction concerning prayer that we do not propose to attempt even a survey of the whole field, but to confine ourselves to the words dealing with the two main lines of responsibility in this matter, those namely, of the practice of prayer personally, and the practice of prayer collectively.

First, as to the former. " But thou, when thou prayest, enter into thine inner chamber, and having shut thy door, pray to thy Father which is in secret, and thy Father which seeth in secret shall recompense thee." We are at once arrested by the " but" with which the passage opens. It makes us conscious of a background, of a contrast which flung the actual words into clearer relief. Immediately preceding Jesus had said, " Ye shall not be as the hypocrites: for they love to stand and pray in the synagogues and in the corners of the streets, that they may be seen of men." Now it is perfectly evident that our Lord did not mean to say it was wrong to stand and pray in the synagogue or at the corner of the street. That against which He warned His disciples was the praying which had as its deepest desire a wish to be seen of men. He charged them to beware of the prayer which obtrudes itself upon human notice. Mark His gentle satire in this respect, " Verily I say unto you, they have their reward." That is to say, they pray to be seen of men, they are seen of men. What they desire, they obtain. This is the background. We are interested in the instructions to which these warnings gave rise. " When thou prayest, enter into thine inner chamber, and having shut thy door, pray to thy Father which is in secret." Thus Christ instructed His disciples that in the life of each one of them there must be a special place, a special time and a special

method, whereby in quietness and loneliness,
every third person being excluded, each one
should pray.

Then as to the latter, " If two of you shall agree
on earth as touching anything they shall ask, it
shall be done for them of My Father which is in
heaven. For where two or three are gathered
together in My name, there am I in the midst of
them." As the first passage insisted upon loneliness, this provides for fellowship in prayer. It
declares the conditions of the true prayer-meeting.
The promise is indeed a spacious one. " If two of
you shall agree on earth as touching anything that
they shall ask, it shall be done for them." It is a
somewhat curious thing that this promise is so
perpetually misquoted by the addition of the
words, " concerning My Kingdom." It may be
said that this, of course, was what our Lord meant
us to understand. I unhesitatingly reply that we
have no right to imagine that He meant anything
other than He said. To introduce these words
is to put a limit upon prayer which He did not
put. If it be objected that this is a dangerous
doctrine, I reply that Christ clearly marked the
limits of such agreement and such asking in the
words, " For where two or three are gathered together in My name, there am I in the midst of
them." The promise is not made to two or three
persons who meet together, and ask simply upon
the basis of their own desire. "Jesus in the midst"
means Jesus enthroned, obeyed, consulted. Where
He is enthroned, obeyed, consulted, the Spirit

creates desire, and prayer. being in harmony with the will of God, the answer is assured. We must neither put false limitations upon this word of the Master, nor must we imagine that there are no limitations. According to Him, the limit is not upon the things for which we may ask, but upon our condition and the Spirit in which we ask. Two or three of us may agree as to our desire for certain things, and may ask for them, and never receive them. The prayer-meeting must not be based upon desire, but upon relationship to Christ. If two or three of us are gathered together in His name, under the dominion of His life, inspired by His Spirit, and if in the hearts of those thus gathered there is created a common desire, then they may ask and be assured of the answer.

These then are the two words of Jesus about prayer which reveal the broad lines of its practice. Firstly that we enter into an inner chamber, shut the door, and pray alone; and secondly, that we gather together two or three in His name and pray. One man may pray alone, indeed he must do so shutting out every other person ; but that does not exhaust the practice of prayer. There must be the prayer-meeting. It is not necessarily a large gathering. The Master names the smallest number that can constitute a meeting—two. There cannot be a meeting of one. Yet the larger number is not necessarily wrong. The indefiniteness of His phrase " two or three " includes the possibility of the larger gathering. That which creates the true prayer-meeting is the inspiration of saints

THE PRACTICE OF PRAYER   109

in communion with each other, because baptized
by the Spirit into living communion with Christ.

Now for the most practical of words concerning
each of these methods. As to the first, I desire to
insist upon the necessity for the formation of very
definite habits. The words of the Master could
not be more emphatic than they are as to the
necessity for separation, seclusion, and secrecy.
An inner chamber and a shut door certainly mean
that there must be in the life of every man or
woman or child a place for retirement, a time for
seclusion, an exercise of this high and holy privi-
lege in absolute loneliness, when husband or wife,
father or mother, brother or sister, son or daughter, is excluded. In all our busy life nothing is of
more importance than that we should have some
place peculiarly consecrated to prayer. The soul
needs a Bethel. It may not be a place retained
exclusively for prayer, but it should be a place to
which at set times we may go and know that we
shall be free from intrusion. For every minister
of the Gospel this Bethel ought to be his study.
I know how constantly we think of the study as
the workroom, and rightly so. Woe be to the
preacher of the Word who is not a workman.
But the study ought to be at times the place
where we may look into the face of God alone
and hold personal communion with Him. This
may sound like a plea for the private oratory of
the Roman Catholic, and so it is in all its deepest
spiritual intention. For the material trappings
of crucifix, picture, or candle I care nothing, but

for the spiritual intention of lonely communion with God in some set place, I care increasingly. There is far more than seems in the place set apart. Those of us who preach the Word surely know what it is to feel the ease of preaching in the place with which one is perfectly familiar. Familiarity enables forgetfulness of surroundings. The "where" matters little. The fact that there is a place is of great importance. To object to the idea of locality is to imagine there was no meaning in the words of Jesus when He spoke of an "inner chamber" and a "shut door." To the merchant, it may be his private office, locked at a certain time for loneliness with God. To the mother it may be the quiet of her own room from which for a little she is able to exclude all those who serve under her in the maintenance of home. It seems to me that if the watchers in the heavenly places observe the places of the sons of men amid earth's conflict, those in which they are most interested are the secret places where the saints hold converse with God. Until we find some place of habitual loneliness made sacred, not by material accessories, but by spiritual access, we are not as strong as we might be, and we have not formed the mightiest habit in the life of prayer. Then it is of equal importance that there should be a special time for prayer. I am perfectly well aware of the answer that comes from thousands of toilers to-day. This is a busy age. Of that there can be no denial, but if the age is too busy to pray, so much the worse for the age; or rather if in the age we are too busy to pray, so much the worse for our business. As to the time of prayer there can be no little doubt that for those who are able the "morning watch" is the finest. Yet I would urge none to be slave of the habit of another. If a proper regard for physical conditions makes it necessary for some over-wrought daughter of the King to rest in the morning hour, let her remember that she is not under law, but under grace. Then let there be no escape from the importance of time by declaring the brevity of the day, and the multiplication of positive duties. In fellowship with God the terms long or short ought to be cancelled. Five minutes with Him in which the soul is touched by the forces of eternity will mean a day full of spiritual vigour. God can do much in five minutes of man's time if no more can honestly be spared. He can do nothing in five minutes for the man who should give Him sixty, who but is slothful. Those who know the value of lonely fellowship with God, at the beginning of the day, know also how hot and restless is the day from which that time of communion has been absent. Again I say, cultivate that method of prayer which is most helpful, whether it be that of speaking aloud in loneliness, or of communing in stillness of heart and silence, whether standing or kneeling or sitting. No special attitude is insisted upon as necessary in the Word of God. The matter of supreme importance is that we discover the method of prayer which helps us most actually to realize the presence of God and hold communion with Him. The place, the time, the method, are matters concerning which there must be individual choice and decision. The matter of supreme importance is the cultivation of the habit of prayer. I do not use the word habit carelessly. Habits need to be formed whether they are good or evil. With regard to prayer that which is at first perhaps somewhat trying and difficult, becomes so much a part of the life as to be not second nature, but first nature. In all these matters it is important to distinguish between the essentials and the accidentals.

It would be disastrous if any should imagine that these set times exhausted the practice of personal prayer. Our Lord declared that " Men ought always to pray, and not to faint," and that is a very profound word. It is evident that His conception of life is that if men pray they will not faint, and conversely, if men do not pray then will they faint. This word indicates the fact that Jesus had a profound consciousness of the pressure and strain of life. He did not think it was a soothing softness through which men glide. To Him life was indeed simple, but also strenuous. He knew that men would be in danger of fainting underneath the burden and in the midst of the battle. He knew also a power which would prevent their fainting. " Men ought always to pray, and not to faint." No man will pray always who neglects the formation of the habit of regular prayer. The disciple who regularly observes a place and time and method will gradually find the habit learned in the secret place is binding also through all the public life. A confirmed habit of regular prayer will create regularity and constancy amidst all irregularities of time and place and method. Prayer in the secret place will create a spirit which will obtain in all public places. Gradually thoughts will become prayers, thoughts of absent friends will take wings and move upwards. Fellowship with God as an activity will issue in fellowship with God as an attitude. When this is so, anywhere, and at any moment, and in any method the spirit will speak its need in the listening ear of God. Our fathers used to speak of and practice ejaculatory prayer. It would be a great gain to all of us if we could learn again the method and practice it. It is a great mistake to imagine that in the midst of London's busy traffic one has to wait for the appointed place and hour and method. It is a great word in the " letter to the Hebrews " which declares that we " may find grace to help us in time of need." I have always felt that I should like to discover some idiom of my own language which would gather the thought of the Greek phrase, and I am not sure but that it is perfectly done by saying that the message declares we may find grace to help us " in the nick of time." The consciousness of this, however, can only be created as we are familiar with the secret place as a result of the set time and place and method.

H

So far we have dealt with only the practice of
prayer in the individual life, with the inner
chamber and the shut door, the special place, the
special time and the special method, and with
prayer flung out in sighs and sentences in the
rush of every-day activity, in the abiding consciousness of God's attention and God's answer.

Turning to the habit of collective prayer,
there is very much that might be said about the
prayer-meeting. The prayer-meeting is a meeting for prayer. That is so obvious a statement
as to appear unnecessary. Yet I do not hesitate
to affirm that there is nothing the Church needs
more at the present hour than to understand
what a real prayer-meeting is. As we have
already briefly said, the perfect ideal is set forth
in the Master's words, "Where two or three are
gathered together in My name, there am I in the
midst of them." He was primarily declaring
the ground upon which He had made His promise
"If two of you shall agree on earth as touching
anything that they shall ask, it shall be done for
them." I am perfectly aware that these sacred
words of our Lord open before our vision vaster
reaches, and have more spacious meanings, but at
the present time we consider them only in the
first application which our Lord made of them.
The first necessity then for the prayer-meeting is
that those constituting it should be gathered "in
His name." Two souls so gathered, each under
His dominion—and the place is of no moment.
The great word "where" is magnificent in its

breadth ; no longer in Jerusalem, no longer at
the temple, no longer in a mountain set apart, no
longer in a church or meeting-house or any other
special place only, but " where," in the home, in
the field, upon the sea, on the mountain, in the
great cathedral, in the mission-hall, they are
" gathered in the Name." We do not catch the
thought if we say " two or three *met* together,"
" *assembled* together," no, they must be " gathered," and the great and only " Gatherer " is the
Lord Himself, acting to-day through the Holy
Spirit. Then they must be gathered " in His
name," which does not merely mean that they
must be called Christians, but they must be
sharers of His nature, those who are living His
life, under the impulse of His love, in the illumination of His light. When such souls are so
gathered you have the prayer-meeting. A meeting for prayer is a meeting of two or three units,
hundreds, thousands, gathered, as we have said,
and who give themselves to prayer. I may be
asked if I would discountenance singing and the
exposition of scripture in prayer-meetings. Well,
I should certainly have no singing in a prayer-
meeting, save the singing of some of the great
prayer hymns of the Church, in which she is
rich. I would have no other reading of the
Word of God save perhaps some passage indicat-
ing our responsibility in or re-stating the charter
of prayer. In the true prayer-meeting there
should be no " waiting." By that I do not mean
that it is necessary always for some one to be en-

gaging in audible prayer, but rather that the cessation of the sounding of a human voice ought not to mean the cessation of prayer. During all the silent pauses, every individual should be in silent communion with God, bearing up quietly some petitions which perhaps have already been decided upon or named in the assembly. Yet on the other hand there should be no "waiting" in the sense of refusing to lead in audible prayer when the Spirit guides. Elder waits for younger, younger waits for elder; the Spirit waits for all, and is grieved and hindered. In the true prayer-meeting there should be preëminently the consciousness that the saints are gathered not only "in His name," but because in His name, in His real presence. Where that is so there will be "waiting" only for direction by the Spirit. It may be objected that this kind of prayer-meeting would not be popular, yet surely it has not come to this that any Christian soul should imagine popularity to be the standard of success in the Church of God.

This habit of collective prayer should not be confined to meetings merely in connection with the Church, that is, on the Church premises. It may be cultivated in the home-life, and indeed everywhere. As an illustration, let me suggest that Christian women should turn their faculty for social entertainment in this direction. Why not have "At Homes" for prayer? At least, they would have the advantage of definiteness, and in that very minor sense would be infinitely superior to many of the unhallowed crushes which characterize so-called social life to-day. Why not issue invitations upon this basis, that your friends should meet in your home to spend an afternoon in prayer. If the so-called friends would not accept the invitation, then surely you, as a Christian, are better without such friends. It is the Church's friendship with people who do not want to pray, which blights the Church and blights the world. The people in the ungodly suburb where your home is, may be, according to the canons of a worldly hour, preëminently respectable, but if they are not prepared to come to your home to talk with Christ, they are injuring you and you are injuring them by your continued friendship. Not only in the home life, but in all social intercourse, the saints should come together more for prayer. I go back in memory to the days when, as a lad at school in Cheltenham, I formed a friendship with one David Smith, a colporteur. His memory is fragrant still. On half-holidays I would accompany him to some of the villages lying among the Cotswold Hills. It was our custom, at his suggestion, to start half an hour earlier than was necessary to bring us in time for the meetings in order that on the way we might make a pause for prayer together. Some of the most hallowed memories of my heart to-day are of those meetings of two, one a young man loving his Lord, and the other a boy, opening his eyes towards the possibility of a life-work, pausing at some stile amid the fields and agreeing together to ask, asking and obtaining answers. The glory of such meetings lies in the utter absence from them of constraint or compulsion of any kind other than that of the presiding Lord. In such a meeting one may pray as many times as the heart prompts. One may stop without elaborate finish, and commence again because in another's prayer a new desire has been born in one's own heart. I think we cannot tell how much it would mean to the strength of the Church if the saints of God cultivated the habit of fellowship in prayer in small groups.

There are three notes of prevailing prayer of which I want to speak briefly. First, definiteness, secondly, importunity, and thirdly, submission. There is nothing we need more in personal prayer than to know what we want, and ask for it. It is possible to waste the great opportunity of prayer by indefiniteness. We may generalize prayer until we vapourize it, and there is no virtue left in it. It is a question whether ministers can serve their churches in any better way than by the simple habit of praying individually for the flock of God committed to their care. During the two years of my ministry at Westminster I have passed from North to South and East to West of my own country, and have twice visited the States. I have gone nowhere during that period without discovering the influence resulting from the ministry of the man of God who built that place, and more than thirty years ago passed on into the light of the Father's home. The

question arises as to what in the life and work of
Samuel Martin created the influence which so
long abides. He was an eloquent preacher, truly,
and a man of saintly character, but perhaps the
greatest thing about him was the fact of his
definite praying. It was his habit to go into that
great building when the doors were shut, and to
pass from pew to pew praying for the people who
occupied them at the regular services of the
church. The same truth applies to our work in
the Sunday-school. There is no more sacred,
holy, or beautiful work than that of the teacher,
no work that needs clearer vision or more tender
heart. Our teachers will find great help from
the practice of definite prayer for their children.
Let them make the register of the scholar's names
a prayer-book in the highest sense of that word.
As every child in turn is born upon the heart,
there will be created a new power for influencing
those thus prayed for towards Christ Himself.

All this is equally true of the collective praying
of the saints. Prayer-meetings have too often
been killed by aimless, rudderless, anchorless
wanderings of such as seem to have no haven. It
would be a habit of great helpfulness if before
prayer the Church decided what it was about to
pray for. It is impossible to pray about everything in one prayer-meeting. One day in a York-
shire prayer-meeting there came a stranger who
did what many men are in the habit of doing—
God forgive them—he made a prayer. When he
had been talking twenty minutes, and no living

man ought to pray in a prayer-meeting above
five, and had been giving the Almighty information of which He had been in possession
long before the man was born, at last he said,
" And now, O Lord God, what more shall we say
unto Thee ? "   An old man who knew how to
pray audibly replied " Call Him ' Feyther,' mon,
and ax for summat."   This principle of definiteness is what we supremely need in individual and
collective praying.   Jesus did not say, " If you
will give God information for twenty minutes in
elegant language you may derive some benefit
therefrom."   He said, " Ask, and receive " ; " seek,
and find " ; "knock, and it shall be opened."

The next note of prevailing prayer is that of
importunity.   In the eleventh and eighteenth
chapters of Luke are two parables which show
this necessity.   The one is a picture of a man who
obtained bread by knocking and by continuing
to knock.   The other is a picture of a woman who
got redress for her wrongs by worrying a judge.
Now Jesus was not teaching that God has to be
begged in order to obtain His favour, not that
He needs to be worried in order to persuade Him
to do right, but rather that it is necessary for our
sakes that there should be importunity.   The man
who asks and forgets does not really feel his need,
and therefore will not receive.   The man who
knocks and runs away will never receive the
beneficence of the One who alone can open the
door.   The men who know the real secret of
prayer knows the meaning also of importunity.

Epaphras agonized in prayer. There must be definiteness, and then importunity.

But importunity must never degenerate into self-will. There must also be submission. Submission as to the form in which the answer shall come; submission as to the method of the answer; submission as to the time of the answer. It must not be forgotten that we cannot see the end from the beginning, cannot understand the ultimate meaning of our own petitions, but we are praying to One who does see the end from the beginning, and who is perfectly conscious of the issue of our petitions. It may be that the things which to us seem most necessary would only prove a hindrance if they were granted. The best answer to such prayer is ever the kindly love which refuses. Therefore there must be submission in all prevailing prayer.

Then as to the subjects of prayer. We are warranted in praying for anything which is within the sphere of the will of God. That statement is inclusive and exclusive. It includes everything which in itself is right, and which forms part of my life and service according to the Divine plan. It excludes everything which is wholly self-centred. There is no doubt that prayer in the Spirit will mean the cessation of a great many petitions. Many things after which we have most strenuously striven even in prayer, we shall be able to strive after no more if our life is responsive to all the facts which make prayer possible. Petitions will be fewer, but they will

be more powerful.   One illustration of exclusion
may be valuable, and yet in giving it let me first
say that I am speaking from my own experience
only.   There may be no application of this illustration to any other.   We must all be perfectly
persuaded in our own minds on such things.
If we have faith we must have it to ourselves before God.   But to return.   I cannot pray as I
once did about the weather.   Who am I that I
should ask that any given day in the calendar
should be fine ?   I am always profoundly thank-
ful that although our friends across the ocean are
able to send us weather forecasts, they do not
send us weather.   God still holds the government
in His own hand.   The mother of a friend of
mine, a Baptist minister, told me why she had
ceased praying concerning this matter.   For many
years at family worship she had been in the habit
of asking for a fine day for the Sunday-school
outing.   When her boy was about ten years of
age he came to her on one such morning and said,
" Mother, I don't think you ought to ask God for
a fine day.   Perhaps it would be a great deal better for the farmers to have it wet, and why
should it be fine just for our outing ? "   She replied that of course her petition was that if it
should be God's will it might be fine.   The boy
then said, " Why don't you ask God to help you
to choose one of His fine days ? "   To me that is
the whole philosophy of praying.   It is not an
arrangement by which we obtain things which
we personally desire.   It is rather the provision

through which we seek to be brought into conformity with the will of God, and to obtain only
the light which enables us to walk therein. Not
that it is wrong to ask definitely, but it is always
wise to carefully weigh our petitions as to
whether or not they really recognize His sover-
eignty and wisdom. Charles Kingsley refused
on one occasion to use the Archbishop's prayer
for the cessation of rain. He recognized that the
long downpour was sorely needed for sanitary
conditions.

There are particular things about which we
ought to pray, for which we are commanded to
pray ; for all the saints, for the Word of God, for
the Christian ministry, for all souls.

Jesus prayed for all the saints in that great in-
tercessory prayer. Paul prayed for these as the
letters of the imprisonment testify. What a healing of our denominational differences would result, if instead of perpetually discussing those
differences we gave ourselves to prayer for each
other.

Then we should pray for the Word of God,
that it " may run and be glorified." Again how
much more powerful such action would be than
that of debating our differing interpretations of
its meaning. Then for the ministry. If the
Church would pray for the ministry instead of
criticising it, there would be wonderful results.
In this connection I should like to urge upon the
Church that its special duty according to the
teaching of the Lord is to pray that God will

thrust out into His harvest His own labourers. I am sometimes asked to appeal to young men to enter the ministry because there is a need of them. My answer is that no man can choose to become a minister—he must be sent. Therefore we should pray as our Master taught us that the Lord Himself will send. In this connection also, it may be well to urge the importance of praying for those who have the sacred and awful charge of training men for the exercise of their ministry. Then moreover, we are to pray for the men who are exercising the holy calling. I once heard Dr. Berry give a charge to a young minister. In the course of that charge he said to the people, "You will get out of my young brother what you expect, and you will expect what you pray for." Then he used this homely but forceful illustration. Said he, "We were giving soup away lately to our poor people, and had issued general instructions that the lads who came to fetch the soup should bring with them a vessel that should hold about two quarts. I was at the soup-kitchen one day, and saw a boy about ten years of age, ragged and dirty, but with eyes that flashed fire, going into the soup-kitchen carrying a vessel that would hold at least three gallons. We could not for shame put two quarts into that." "Now," said Dr. Berry, "when you come to hear your minister, do not bring a two-quart measure!" Oh, what it is to preach to men and women who have been praying for you.

Then we are charged to pray for all souls, the

sorrowing, the sighing, the sad, the sinning.
Moreover there is no small matter about which
we have not the right to pray.   Anna Shipton
wrote a little book called *Tell Jesus*, being the
memorials of Emily Goss.   It is the story of a
girl who told Jesus everything, from the trouble
of a tangle in a skein of wool to the joys of the
passing hours.

From this sacred service of prayer no saint of
God is excluded ; the youngest and the weakest
can pray.   There are some of us who are excluded from certain lines of service because of
the pressure of life upon us, but no one of us is
excluded from prayer.   There are saints of God
who for long, long years have been shut off from
all the activities of the Church, and even from the
worship of the sanctuary, but who, nevertheless,
have continued to labour together in prayer with
the whole fellowship of the saints.   There comes
to me the thought of one woman who, to my
knowledge, since 1872 in this great babel of London, has been in perpetual pain, and yet in constant prayer.   She is to-day a woman twisted
and distorted by suffering, and yet exhaling the
calm and strength of the secret of the Most
High.   In 1872 she was a bed-ridden girl in the
North of London, praying that God would send
revival to the Church of which she was a member, and yet into which even then she never came.
She had read in the little paper called *Revival*,
which subsequently became *The Christian*, the
story of a work being done in Chicago among

ragged children by a man called Moody. She
had never seen Moody, but putting that little paper under her pillow, she began to pray, "O Lord,
send this man to our Church." She had no means
of reaching him or communicating with him.
He had already visited the country in 1867, and
in 1872 he started again for a short trip with no
intention of doing any work. Mr. Lessey, however, the pastor of the church of which this girl
was a member, met him and asked him to preach
for him. He consented, and after the evening
service he asked those who would decide for
Christ to rise, and hundreds did so. He was surprised, and imagined that his request had been
misunderstood. He repeated it more clearly, and
again the response was the same. Meetings were
continued throughout the following ten days, and
four hundred members were taken into the
church. In telling me this story Moody said, "I
wanted to know what this meant. I began
making inquiries and never rested until I found
a bed-ridden girl praying that God would bring
me to that Church. He had heard her, and
brought me over four thousand miles of land and
sea in answer to her request." This story is told
in the life of D. L. Moody by his son: but now
let me continue it. That girl was a member of
my church when I was pastor at New Court.
She is still a member, still suffering, still confined
to her own room. When in 1901 I was leaving
England for America I went to see her. She
said to me, "I want you to reach that birthday

book." I did so and turning to February 5 I saw
in the handwriting I knew so well, " *D. L. Moody,
Psalm 91.*" Then Marianne Adlard said to me,
" He wrote that for me when he came to see me
in 1872, and I prayed for him every day till he
went home to God." Continuing, she said, " Now,
will you write your name on your birthday page,
and let me pray for you until either you or I go
home." I shall never forget writing my name
in that book. To me the room was full of the
Presence. I have often thought of that hour in
the rush of busy life, in the place of toil and
strain, and even yet by God's good grace I know
that Marianne Adlard is praying for me, and it is
for this reason that to her in sincere love and ad-
miration I have dedicated this book. These are
the labourers of force in the fields of God. It
is the heroes and heroines who are out of sight,
and who labour in prayer, who make it possible
for those who are in sight to do their work and
win. The force of it to such as are called upon
to exercise the ministry can never be measured.

The personal word must again be forgiven. I
never stand up in any assembly at home or
abroad without knowing that three people nearer
to me than any others will pray for me, my wife,
my mother and my father. Oh, the power of it,
and the humbling of it! It makes a man feel
that he must be in line with such praying, and he
is afraid. Yet it makes him strong for he knows
that " more things are wrought by prayer than
this world dreams of." Oh, for the multiplica-

tion of those who will devote themselves to this special labour of intercession.

With all that we have attempted to consider in our minds, we lift our faces to the face of our Lord as did the men who watched Him pray in the olden days, and say to Him, "Lord, teach us to pray."